More Praise for *The Outward Mindset*

"The Outward Mindset is a thought-provoking, game-changing book. Filled with vivid, real-life examples, it argues clearly and persuasively for a better way of doing business."

—Gene McCarthy, President and CEO, ASICS America

"Anyone interested in restoring the public's trust in cops must use the principles of this book as the foundation of that effort. I cannot imagine any situation where this book should not be mandatory reading."

—Jon Hamm, CEO, California Association of Highway Patrolmen

"The Outward Mindset powerfully demonstrates how teams can come together to deliver superior results. I had a hard time putting it down and, applying the frameworks myself, have seen an immediate, practical impact."

—Dan Shimoff, Vice President, McGraw-Hill Education

"Along with all of Arbinger's work, this book is not just foundational but transformational, and not just business changing but life changing."

—John Fikany, Vice President of Strategy, Quicken Loans, Inc.

"This book is a must-read for those who want to know how to make a big difference in the lives of the people they lead and the results they achieve. It will change how you approach the challenges in your company, community, and family."

—Elizabeth Hall, former Vice President, Human Resources, Cricket Communications

"The new perspective provided by this book and its built-in practical application tools have motivated me to actively experiment. I'm amazed at how quickly conversations, reactions, and behaviors are changing for the better."

—Gary M. Riding, Senior Vice President, Samsung Electronics America

"Another gift from Arbinger! At once practical and transformational."

—Craig Tingey, Principal Advisor, Leadership Development, Rio Tinto

"The Outward Mindset completely transforms approaches to culture change and change management. It is a very important book."

—Roberto Sánchez Romero, Global Head of Culture and Values, Everis

"*The Outward Mindset* provides a compelling framework for self-accountability. It is a must-read for leaders who are looking to mobilize themselves, their teams, or their organizations to achieve a collective goal."

—Nancy Murphy, Executive Director, Learning Operations, Cox Communications

"Leaders who serve others with an outward mindset encourage a culture of collaboration where everybody wins. Read *The Outward Mindset* and learn how great servant leaders think."

—Ken Blanchard, coauthor of *The New One Minute Manager* and *Collaboration Begins with You*

"*The Outward Mindset* is so readable and entertaining that its powerful substance will sneak up on you. It's packed with engaging stories and a clear, compelling, and practical message. As with Arbinger's prior work, the principles in this book are foundational and can indeed *change lives and transform organizations.*"

—Van Zeck, former Commissioner of the Public Debt, US Department of the Treasury

"An outward mindset is essential for empowering human potential and possibility. It unlocks an organization's ability to preserve and grow profitability with limited resources."

—Jeff Kerr, Executive Vice President, U.S. Bank

"Superb writing and clear, cogent thinking on a critically important topic. This book will help individuals, organizations, and families."

—Robert Daines, Pritzker Professor of Law and Business, Stanford Law School

"The authentic and engaging storytelling in *The Outward Mindset* makes it a quick and easy read, with real-life lessons that show that taking care of the needs of others is not only the right thing to do but good business as well."

—Benjamin Karsch, Executive Vice President and Chief Marketing Officer, Revlon

"*The Outward Mindset* details a kind of radical presence with others that transforms relationships, enriches lives, and boosts organizational performance. It scores a rare trifecta—important, engaging, and practically powerful."
—**Corey Jamison, President and CEO, XperienceU Training and Leadership Development**

"Through practical real-life examples, *The Outward Mindset* shows how personal and organizational transformations occur when we look beyond ourselves to the needs of others. The concepts are transformational for any type or size of organization."
—**Dave Friedman, Chief of Staff, Office of the CEO, Citrix**

"A thought-provoking and practical book! It helps me look at my personal and professional life with a whole new perspective."
—**Tom DiDonato, Senior Vice President, Human Resources, Lear Corporation**

"This book vividly illustrates the tangible benefits of an outward mindset both at work and at home. It has filled me with hope and motivated me to do better than I have been doing."
—**Rod Larson, CEO, Spandex**

"*The Outward Mindset* is a 'how to' field guide for promoting personal and organizational mindset change—which, more than changes to process or anything else, is the change that actually yields results."
—**Neil McDonough, President and CEO, FLEXcon**

"Simple but meaningful concepts applicable to work and home. Hits the nail on the head in prioritizing mindset change over leader behaviors."
—**Simon Kelner, Global Head of Talent Development, Merck**

"*The Outward Mindset* is an easy-to-digest essential guide for all—beginning with CEOs and other leaders, whose most important responsibility is to see everything through the lens of an outward mindset and to help others do the same."
—**Alistair Cameron, CEO, ASICS EMEA**

"In today's complex, fast-paced environment, an outward mindset is critical to success. This book shows how individuals and organizations can achieve such a mindset change. I highly recommend it."
—**Rick Dreher, Managing Partner, Wipfli, LLP**

"An outward mindset is the foundation of leadership effectiveness. All relationships depend on it."
—**Brad Botteron, CEO, Wachter, Inc.**

"An interesting and engaging approach to effect lasting change in organizations—one that conceivably lends itself to applications in diplomacy as well. *The Outward Mindset* is bound to be a winner for the organizations and leaders that adopt it."
—**Emanuel Shahaf, CEO, Technology Asia Consulting Ltd.**

"*The Outward Mindset* merits deep reflection and attention both personally and organizationally."
—**Joe Farrow, Commissioner, California Highway Patrol**

"*The Outward Mindset* is a must-read for anyone wanting to create personal and organizational excellence."
—**Pierce Murphy, Director, Office of Professional Accountability, City of Seattle**

"*The Outward Mindset* captures the skills needed to lead agencies in the rapidly changing environment that we are all facing."
—**Chris Connally, Chief of Police, St. Joseph Police Department**

"This book gets to the core issues of organizational behavior in a way I've never seen. I aspire to be more like the individuals in this book who are making such a profound impact by focusing on how they can help others achieve their goals."
—**Lindsay Hadley, Executive Producer, 2012 and 2013 Global Citizen Festival**

"Transformational! An outward mindset guarantees better results and a better life."
—**Jean-François Turgeon, President, Tronox**

"Any organization that strives for improvement, teamwork, and world-class results can gain a significant advantage by applying *The Outward Mindset* principles. As a bonus the book will help with personal relationships too!"
—**Bob Miller, Global Client Director, IBM**

THE OUT-WARD MIND SET

THE OUT-WARD MIND SET

How to Change Lives and Transform Organizations

THE ARBINGER INSTITUTE

BK

Berrett-Koehler Publishers, Inc.

Berrett-Koehler Publishers, Inc.
1333 Broadway, Suite 1000
Oakland, CA 94612-1921
Tel: (510) 817-2277
Fax: (510) 817-2278
www.bkconnection.com

ORDERING INFORMATION

Quantity sales. Special discounts are available on quantity purchases by corporations, associations, and others. For details, contact the "Special Sales Department" at the Berrett-Koehler address above.

Individual sales. Berrett-Koehler publications are available through most bookstores. They can also be ordered directly from Berrett-Koehler: Tel: (800) 929-2929; Fax: (802) 864-7626; www.bkconnection.com.

Orders for college textbook / course adoption use. Please contact Berrett-Koehler: Tel: (800) 929-2929; Fax: (802) 864-7626.

Distributed to the U.S. trade and internationally by Penguin Random House Publisher Services.

Berrett-Koehler and the BK logo are registered trademarks of Berrett-Koehler Publishers, Inc.

Printed in the United States of America.

Berrett-Koehler books are printed on long-lasting acid-free paper. When it is available, we choose paper that has been manufactured by environmentally responsible processes. These may include using trees grown in sustainable forests, incorporating recycled paper, minimizing chlorine in bleaching, or recycling the energy produced at the paper mill.

Library of Congress Cataloging-in-Publication Data

Names: Arbinger Institute, issuing body.
Title: The outward mindset : how to change lives and transform
  organizations / The Arbinger Institute.
Description: Expanded second edition. | Oakland, CA : Berrett-Koehler
  Publishers, [2019] | Includes bibliographical references and index.
Identifiers: LCCN 2019018736 | ISBN 9781523087303 (print paperback)
Subjects: LCSH: Organizational behavior. | Organizational change. |
  Attitude (Psychology) | Change (Psychology)
Classification: LCC HD58.7 .O89 2019 | DDC 650.1–dc23
LC record available at https://lccn.loc.gov/2019018736
Second Edition

29 28 27 26 25 24 23 22 21 20 19   10 9 8 7 6 5 4 3 2

Cover designer: Michael Brown

How much larger your life would be
if your self could become smaller in it.

G. K. CHESTERTON

CONTENTS

PREFACE

At long last, leaders are recognizing the link between performance and mindset and beginning to study and apply mindset change strategies. Mindset has always been a fundamental driver of personal and organizational success, but a presumption in modern culture in favor of behavioral approaches to change has until recently obscured from popular view the foundational nature of mindset. The fog is now lifting.

People often use *mindset* to refer to a core belief about oneself, but our work at the Arbinger Institute shows that this is too narrow a focus. The biggest lever for change is not a change merely in self-belief but a fundamental change in the way people see and regard their connections and obligations to others. *The Outward Mindset* explores why this is the case and how to systematically go about building in oneself and one's team or organization the kind of mindset that best enables personal and organizational growth and performance.

Drawing on over four decades of research and three decades of successfully applying that research with Arbinger Institute clients around the world, this book presents our findings about mindset in both theoretical and immediately practical ways. Human beings are inescapably together—mutually affecting and being affected by others. As you will discover, the mutual impact people have on one another turns on whether they carry a self-focused inward mindset or an others-inclusive outward mindset. Understanding the dynamics of this mutual reciprocity and what to do to improve it is the focus of this book.

On many occasions, Richard Sheridan, software engineering pioneer and CEO of Menlo Innovations, has called the ideas in this book *the operating system of the soul*. An understanding of that operating system will enable you to make personal and organizational changes much more effectively than you've been able until now. It will help you become more outward in your work, your leadership, and your life. It will guide you in building more innovative and collaborative teams and organizations. And it will help you see why you admire many of the people you do and what you can do to become more like them.

The Outward Mindset follows our previous international bestsellers, *Leadership and Self-Deception* and *The Anatomy of Peace*. It reflects the Arbinger Institute's latest work on mindset change and shows specifically how to move individuals, teams, families, and entire organizations from inward to outward mindsets. This second edition includes two new chapters. The new chapter 3 outlines where Western philosophical thought has gone wrong with respect to mindset and the resulting problems those mistakes have created in modern approaches to self-help and leadership. The new chapter 17 explores how to implement a game plan for turning mindsets outward.

Whereas our earlier books unfold as fictional stories, *The Outward Mindset* is composed of multiple real-life stories— most of them from our clients. Most chapters are built around one or more such stories. Where context suggests anonymity, we have changed names and details to obscure identities.

In comparing the effectiveness of organizational-change efforts between companies that focus only on behavior change as compared to those that focus on changing both behavior and mindset, a recent McKinsey & Company study found that organizations that identify and address pervasive mindsets at the outset are "four times more likely to succeed in organizational-change efforts than are companies that overlook this stage."[1] Our hope for you, the reader, is that this book will equip you to become substantially more effective in your improvement efforts as well.

PART I
WHY MINDSET MATTERS

1. A DIFFERENT APPROACH

Two black cargo vans snake down Wabash Avenue in Kansas City, Missouri. The passengers are members of the Kansas City Police Department (KCPD) SWAT team. They are about to serve a high-risk drug warrant—the fifth warrant service of that day. The targets of this warrant are sufficiently dangerous that the squad has obtained a "no-knock" warrant, meaning that they will storm through the door unannounced. The men are dressed in black from head to toe, their faces covered by masks that leave only their eyes exposed. Bullet-resistant helmets and body armor make them an intimidating sight.

Senior Sergeant Charles "Chip" Huth, who had been leader of the 1910 SWAT Squad for eight years, is driving the lead van. He slows as the target residence comes into view, and his men stream from both vehicles as quietly and quickly as they can.

Three officers sprint around to the back of the house and take cover, supplying containment should the targets attempt to flee. Seven others, including Chip, run to the front door, six of them with their guns drawn. The seventh runs a well-used battering ram up to the door and slams it through.

"Police," they yell. "Everybody down!" Inside is bedlam. Men attempt to scramble out of the room, some to the stairs and others down hallways. Young children stand as if paralyzed, screaming. A number of women cower in terror on the floor, some of them shielding infants who are screaming at the top of their lungs.

Two of the men—the two suspects, it turns out—go for their weapons but are taken down by officers. "Don't even think about it!" the officers shout. Then they pull the men's arms behind them and put them in cuffs.

With all the young children, the scene in this home is more hectic than most, but within five minutes, the two suspects lie facedown on the living-room floor, and the rest of the inhabitants have been gathered into the dining room.

With everyone's safety secured, the officers begin their search. They move with purpose and precision. Chip notices his point man, Bob Evans, leaving the room, and he assumes Bob is simply joining the search.

A couple of minutes later, Chip passes the kitchen as he walks down the hall. Bob is standing at the kitchen sink. A moment earlier, Bob had been rifling through the kitchen cabinets looking for white powder—not for contraband to be used as evidence against those they are arresting but for a white powder that was of much greater immediate importance. He was looking for Similac. With babies crying and their mothers understandably in hysterics, this most alpha male of all the alpha males on Chip's squad was looking for a way to help them. When Chip sees him, Bob is mixing baby bottles.

Bob looks at Chip with a faint smile and shrugs. He then picks up the bottles and begins distributing them to the mothers of the crying infants. Chip is delighted by this. He hadn't thought of baby bottles himself, but he completely understands what Bob is up to and why.

This one act of responsiveness changes the entire scene. Everyone calms down, and Chip and his men are able to explain the situation thoroughly and then smoothly turn the two suspects over to the detectives. Nevertheless, mixing baby bottles is such an unusual and unpredictable act that many people in police work—including the members of this SWAT team just a few years earlier—would have considered it irrational. But in Chip's squad, this kind of responsiveness is routine.

It wasn't always this way. To appreciate the remarkable transformation that had come to the 1910 SWAT Squad, we need to learn a little of Chip's challenging background and his history in the Kansas City Police Department.

Chip was born in 1970, the son of an alcoholic, abusive career criminal and a bipolar, schizophrenic mother. When Chip's father was around, the family usually was running from the law—moving from state to state around the South. When his father was absent, Chip, his siblings, and their mother often lived out of a car, collecting cans and cardboard for recycling as a way to survive.

One time when his father returned, promising that things would be different, his abuse of the family escalated. Chip, age ten at the time, stood up to him, and this finally prompted Chip's mother to call the one person her husband feared—her ex–Special Forces brother, who came to wrest the family away from the man. "I'm here to get my sister and the kids," he told Chip's father. "If you get up off that couch, it's going to be the last thing you ever do." That was the last time Chip saw his father.

Chip's father hated cops, which is the primary reason Chip became one. He joined KCPD in 1992. After three years as a patrol officer, he was moved to a SWAT team. Four years later, he joined the police academy as a use-of-force and firearms instructor. He was promoted to SWAT sergeant in 2004. The chief of police thought that the 1910 and 1920 SWAT Squads, which act as the strong arm of the Investigations Bureau of the police department, were out of control. Chip came in as a hatchet man to fix them.

What the chief may not have known, however, was that at the time, Chip was psychologically better suited to *lead* such a group than he was to change it. He made sure to outwork all his men so that he could kick their butts if necessary. Whenever he felt threatened, he responded with threats of violence, and he was just unstable enough that his team members were kept in line.

He was even more severe with the public. The way he saw things, there really are bad guys in the world (he should know since he grew up with one), and they need to be dealt with in a way that makes them sorry they ever committed a crime. Everyone the team members arrested, they took down *hard*. And they didn't much care how they treated people's property or pets. It wasn't uncommon for some of Chip's men to spit tobacco on suspects' furniture, for example, or to put a bullet through the skull of a potentially dangerous dog.

Chip's squad was one of the most complained-about units in KCPD. Some of that was to be expected, since SWAT officers tend to do more damage than regular officers on the street. But even so, the rate of complaints against the squad was alarming, and the cost of the associated litigation was a drain on the department. Chip didn't see a problem with this. He believed his squad was working with people in the only way it could. In fact, he thought the more complaints he and his squad received, the more proof they had that they were doing something right!

A couple of years after Chip took over the SWAT squad, another KCPD officer, Jack Colwell, helped Chip see some truths about himself that startled him—about the person Chip had become and how his attitude and methods were actually undercutting his effectiveness and putting his men and their missions at risk. This revelation coincided with a troubling encounter Chip had with his fifteen-year-old son. Driving his son home from school one day, Chip could tell that something was on his mind and began asking question after question of his son, with no response. "Why won't you tell me what's bothering you?" Chip asked. "You wouldn't understand," his son responded. "Why?" Chip asked. "Why do you think I wouldn't understand?" Then his son gave Chip the answer that perhaps prepared him to hear what Jack had to say: "Because you're a robot, Dad."

This comment cut deep. Chip began thinking about the kind of person he had become. He had believed that suspicion and aggression were necessary for survival and success in a vicious, combative, and violent world. But now he started to see that being this kind of person did not put a stop to the viciousness and combat; it actually accelerated it.

These events started Chip on a journey of change, an endeavor that resulted in a complete transformation of the work of his squad. The team used to receive two to three complaints a month, many of them regarding excessive use of force. On average, these complaints cost the department $70,000 per incident. However, because of the team members' new way of working, they haven't had a complaint filed against them in twelve years. It is rare, now, that they leave others' personal property in shambles or shoot a dog. They even hired a dog specialist to teach them ways to control potentially dangerous animals. And they never spit tobacco. Chip told his men, "Unless you can tell me that chewing tobacco in people's homes advances the mission, we're not doing that anymore." And, of course, they prepare baby bottles.

These changes have increased the cooperation Chip and his team receive from suspects and from the community, and the results have been astounding. In addition to shrinking community complaints against them to zero, in the first three years after adopting this approach, the 1910 SWAT Squad recovered more illegal drugs and guns than it had in the previous decade.

What transformed the team's approach and effectiveness? A different kind of mindset than the members ever had before: a way of seeing and thinking that we call an *outward mindset*.

Mark Ballif and Paul Hubbard, co-CEOs of a highly respected healthcare company, have built their organization utilizing an outward-mindset approach similar to the one Chip has used with his squad. A few years ago, they were meeting with the principals of a venerable private equity firm in New York City. With 32 percent and 30 percent compound annual growth rates in top-line revenue and profitability, respectively, over the prior five years, getting meetings like this one with potential capital investors hadn't been difficult for Mark and Paul.

"So you have turned around over fifty healthcare facilities?" the firm's managing partner asked.

Mark and Paul nodded.

"How?"

Mark and Paul looked at each other, waiting for the other to answer. "It all hinges on finding and developing the right leaders," Mark finally said.

"And what is the most important qualification you look for in a leader?" Mark and Paul felt as if they were being cross-examined.

"Humility," Paul answered. "That's what distinguishes those who can turn these facilities around from those who can't.

Leaders who succeed are those who are humble enough to be able to see beyond themselves and perceive the true capacities and capabilities of their people. They don't pretend to have all the answers. Rather, they create an environment that encourages their people to take on the primary responsibility for finding answers to the challenges they and their facilities face."

The other members of the equity firm in the meeting looked at the managing partner, who sat poker-faced.

"Humility?" he finally said, his tone condescending. "You're telling me that you've acquired fifty failing facilities and turned each of them around by finding leaders who have *humility?*"

"Yes," Mark and Paul replied without hesitation.

The managing partner stared at them for a moment. Then he pushed his chair back from the table and rose to his feet. "That doesn't compute to me." Without even a handshake, he turned and strode out of the room, leaving behind a compelling investment opportunity in a company with a proven track record. What he couldn't comprehend was how the company's results depended on humble leaders who "see beyond themselves," as Paul had described.

Nearly fifteen years earlier, Mark, Paul, and another early partner decided to try their hand at building their own company. They had less than ten years of experience in healthcare between them, but they saw an opportunity to create a unique organization in an industry plagued with problems. So they began purchasing the clinically and financially beleaguered facilities their competitors were desperate to be rid of. They were convinced that the key missing ingredient in failing healthcare operations was not an absence of the right people or even the right location but an absence of the right mindset. They engaged in a systematic approach to apply the principles that are presented in this book.

Mark explains their experience this way: "Some of our competition couldn't get rid of facilities and their teams fast enough because they thought that the teams were simply defective. Our thesis was that we could take a poorly led and therefore underperforming facility and, by helping the existing team see what was possible, *they* could turn it around."

As they acquired their first facilities, they encountered a pattern that would repeat itself, almost without exception, acquisition after acquisition. The outgoing leader, trying to do them a favor, would give them a list of the five or so staff members they would need to fire if they stood any chance of turning things around. "We would thank them for the list and then go to work," Mark and Paul reminisced. "Invariably, four of the five people would turn out to be our best performers."

Consider what this demonstrates. If those who had been identified as problems could, when working under new leadership and a new approach, become star performers, then organizational improvement, even turnaround, is less a matter of getting the wrong people off the bus than a matter of helping people see. It is a matter of changing mindset.

"Leaders fail," Paul explains, "by coming in saying, 'Here's the vision. Now you go execute what I see.' That's just wrong in our view of the world." Continuing, he says, "Although leaders should provide a mission or context and point toward what is possible, what humble, good leaders *also* do is to help people see. When people see, they are able to exercise all their human agency and initiative. When they do that, they own their work. When people are free to execute what they see, rather than simply to enact the instructions of the leader, they can change course in the moment to respond to ever-changing, situation-specific needs. That kind of nimbleness and responsiveness is something you can't manage, force, or orchestrate."

Mark and Paul learned these lessons early on as they operated their first few facilities themselves. Reading situations attentively, they found themselves mixing plenty of baby bottles—taking responsibility to do whatever each situation required. As they acquired more facilities, they needed other leaders who could operate with an outward mindset—people who would mix baby bottles as necessary and help others learn to do the same.

This book is about how to help unlock this kind of collaboration, innovation, and responsiveness—how to experience a way of seeing, thinking, working, and leading that helps individuals, teams, and organizations significantly improve performance.

At first, you might feel like the private equity firm leader who walked out of the meeting with Mark and Paul. The ideas we will cover may not make perfect sense to you early on, and you might wonder whether these concepts can help you with the challenges you are currently facing. We invite you to stay in the meeting. You will learn an actionable, repeatable, and scalable way to transform your personal, team, and organizational performance.

Just as importantly, you will begin seeing situations outside of work differently as well. You will see new and better ways to interact with those you care most about, including those you find most difficult. Everything in this book that applies to people in organizations applies to people in their home and family lives as well—and vice versa. This is why we include corporate, home, and individual stories. Lessons learned from each will apply across the board.

Our journey begins with an idea that Chip, Mark, and Paul believe to be foundational: *mindset drives and shapes all that we do — how we engage with others and how we behave in every moment and situation.*

2. WHAT DRIVES PERFORMANCE

Given external realities, achievement is driven by two things, one of which is well understood and one of which is not. The obvious contributing factor to success is a person's actions or behaviors—the things one chooses to do. Most modern approaches to success treat this *first* success factor—behavior—as if it were the *only* factor to success. Even while acknowledging that other factors such as attitudes and values also matter, people who believe in a purely behavioral approach to performance end up recommending behavioral formulas for improving attitudes or defining values. For behaviorists, all problems—and therefore, all solutions—are behavioral.

You might wonder what is wrong with this, as the idea that behaviors drive results is almost self-evident. You might argue (rightfully, in our view) that focusing on behavior change is beneficial since the *observability* of behaviors allows one to measure progress by measuring whether or not key behaviors are changing. Our work over three decades of helping client organizations improve their performance confirms the importance of focusing on improving behaviors. The collective behaviors of an organization's members do, in fact, drive the organization's results. And the same is true for individuals: their behaviors drive their achievements (as well as their failures).

To understand why a purely behavioral approach to human performance is nevertheless problematic, let's consider two cases. The first case is the story we shared in chapter 1 about Chip Huth and his SWAT squad. Their story is powerful in part because it is so surprising. We don't imagine SWAT officers stopping in the middle of an operation to mix baby bottles. It's not just that most SWAT officers would choose not to mix baby bottles; it's that the very idea would never occur to them in the first place. Why not? Because it is not an idea that would spring from the prevailing mindsets of most people who operate in that kind of role. The way we use the term, *mindset* is more than a belief about oneself. It refers to the way people see and regard the world — how they see circumstances, challenges, opportunities, other people, and themselves. Their behaviors are always a function of how they see their situations, relationships, and possibilities.

Consider what this story reveals: while it is true that behaviors drive outcomes, it is also true that another factor — mindset — determines what behavioral options will occur to a person in the first place *and* what behavioral choices one will then make from among those options. So while it's true that behavior drives results, it's also true that mindset drives behavior. Consequently, any solution to human problems that ignores this reality ignores too much of what's true to produce reliable results.

Approaches that ignore the importance of mindset fail to account for not only why people are choosing to behave as they do but also why people respond as they do to others. To illustrate this, consider a second story.

A person we'll call Mia attends a workshop on improving communication. Over the course of two days, she learns an array of new skills. She learns to ask more open and inviting questions. She is taught how to respond when someone becomes verbally aggressive or, on the other hand, when someone becomes evasive or completely shuts down. She practices paraphrasing what others say to demonstrate that she is paying attention. She learns to use more tentative language to invite better responses from others. She also learns how to offer better nonverbal cues: presenting a pleasant look and demeanor, maintaining better eye contact, and so on.

Mia returns to work determined to put her learning into practice. In particular, she wants to see if these skills will help her in her interactions with a colleague named Carl, with whom she has struggled. The truth is that she very much dislikes and distrusts Carl. She tenses up whenever he is around.

What do you think is likely to happen when Mia begins to apply these new skills in her conversations with Carl? Could Mia's behavioral changes make her seem so different to Carl that their interactions will significantly improve as a result? Perhaps. However, Mia is likely to feel different *to* Carl only to the extent that she actually feels differently *about* Carl, regardless of what new skills she uses or behaviors she adopts.

If Mia feels the same way about Carl as she always has, and if Carl senses this, he might begin to wonder what Mia is up to. He might even get upset, feeling that Mia is trying to hide significant issues beneath a veneer of superficial change.

If Carl were to respond to Mia in this way, one would say that the new behaviors Mia adopted ended up not making much of a difference. In fact, the whole experience could even *increase* the tension between them. Mia's new and better skills could result in *worse* outcomes rather than better outcomes.

This doesn't mean that Mia's new skills were damaging in and of themselves. It does suggest, however, that something in addition to behavior plays an essential role in both our successes and our failures. And if that's true, then the effectiveness of our behaviors depends to some significant degree on something that is deeper than behavior.

So we are suggesting two core problems with a purely behavioral approach for improving performance:

1. As in Chip's experience with the baby bottles, the behaviors people choose to engage in (that they sense are right and helpful given their situation) will depend on how they see their situation and those with whom they interact. So while behaviors drive results, behaviors themselves are informed and shaped by one's mindset.

2. As in Mia's story, in whatever a person does, his or her mindset comes through, and others respond to this combination of behavior *and* mindset. This means that the effectiveness of an individual's behaviors will depend to some significant degree on that individual's mindset.

We capture these realities in diagram 1: the mindset model. In the area of organizational change, what does the mindset model suggest? It at least suggests that change efforts built upon the incomplete behavioral approach, where a person or organization tries to improve performance by focusing only on behavior change, will fail much more often in comparison to efforts that focus on changing both behavior *and* mindset.

Studies conducted by McKinsey & Company corroborate this. One study finds that "failure to recognize and shift mindsets can stall the change efforts of an entire organization."[1] A second McKinsey study finds that organizations that "identify and address pervasive mindsets at the outset are four times more likely to succeed in organizational-change efforts than are

DIAGRAM 1. **THE MINDSET MODEL**

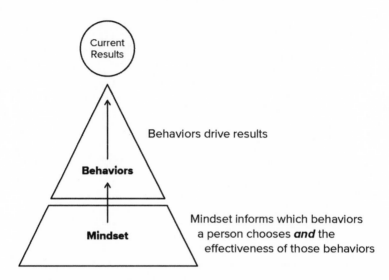

companies that overlook this stage."[2] Think about that. Those who attempt to effect change by concentrating on changing mindsets are *four times* more likely to succeed than those who focus only on changing behavior.

With these findings in mind, consider two different performance-improvement approaches. In the first approach, a person or organization attempts to push behavior change while neglecting mindset change, as shown in diagram 2 on the next page.

If a person or company tries to get people to adopt new behaviors that aren't supported by their underlying mindsets, how successful do you think such a change effort will be?

In response to this question, one executive we were meeting with said, "Some leaders, through charisma, willpower, or constant micromanaging, may be able to drive this kind of change in

DIAGRAM 2. **THE BEHAVIOR-PUSH APPROACH**

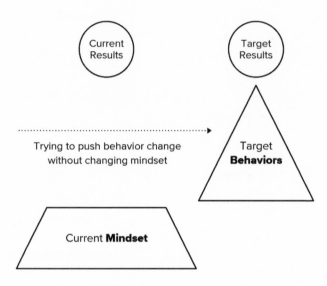

the short term, even without an accompanying degree of mindset change. But in my experience, it won't last. When that leader leaves, if not sooner, things will snap back to where they were."

Others in the meeting agreed. "Without a change in the prevailing mindset in an organization," one of them said, "behavior-change efforts tend to be resisted. While 'compliant' behavior by employees might be achievable, at least to some degree, 'committed' behavior won't happen without a change in mindset. And it's *committed* behavior that makes the biggest difference."

Is the same thing true in your experience? In your work life and in your home life, what have you noticed happens (or doesn't happen) when people try to push behavior change in a culture where the mindset remains unchanged?

Contrast the behavior-push approach with an approach that includes a focus on mindset change. Diagram 3 shows the approach Chip initiated within his SWAT squad when he started working on mindset change.

A focus on mindset change among Chip's team members led to dramatic improvements in their behaviors and results. As their story illustrates, when you sufficiently improve the mindset— either of an individual or of an organization—you no longer have to specify everything each team member is supposed to do (the way those who operate from a behavioral model often assume). As the mindset changes, so does the behavior, *without having to prescribe the change.* And where certain behaviors still need to be stipulated, the suggestions won't be systematically resisted.

DIAGRAM 3. **THE LEADING-WITH-MINDSET APPROACH**

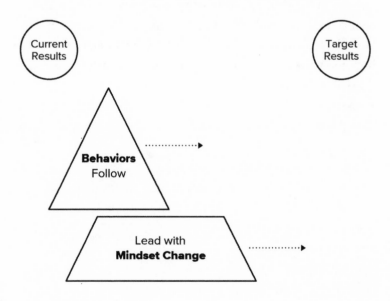

For these reasons, mindset change facilitates sustainable behavior change.

Moreover, as their mindsets change, people begin thinking and acting in ways they hadn't imagined before. Chip, for example, had never thought about a scenario where his team might need to prepare baby bottles to help mothers calm screaming children. Consequently, he'd never taught or mentioned this to his team. However, because he had put in the effort to establish a different mindset in the members of his team (beginning with his own), he didn't have to think about or mandate it in advance. When this new and unanticipated situation came up, one of his men thought of the right thing to do on his own. The underlying mindset prompted the most helpful behaviors in the moment.

Most approaches to leadership share two common problems. As we've discussed in this chapter, they fail to account adequately for mindset and therefore put too much faith in our ability to change behavior without addressing mindset. In addition, however, a problem that originated in Western thought some four hundred years ago has led to mindset and leadership approaches that are built on a mistake.

3.   ISOLATED OR TOGETHER?

The father of modern philosophy, René Descartes, made assumptions that have so saturated Western culture since his time that few people even realize the premises they have accepted. Descartes's presumptions are part of the cultural air we now breathe. In this chapter, we will explore a problem with that cultural air—a mistake about the nature of the self that has infected modern leadership and self-help theories. That mistake is the widely accepted conception of the self as an inherently separate and isolated entity independent from others. As we will explain, such a "self" doesn't actually exist. People are at once independent and dependent, both alone and fundamentally together, at the same time influencing others and being influenced by them. Our connections with others are integral to who we are. As a result, mindsets and leadership practices that discount this reality create many interpersonal and organizational problems.

Let's begin by considering a few of the ways human beings are fundamentally connected with each other. No one gives birth to oneself, of course, which means that life itself depends on other people. The creation of life, too, takes more than one person. And then consider how human bodies, which seem to belong to people individually, actually are made up of the genetic histories and markers of those who have come before. As a result, although a person's weight, for example, depends in part on how much one eats and exercises, the genetic predisposition one inherits from others has a significant impact as well.

This means that our bodies depend on other people—for their existence, their properties, and to some significant extent, even their abilities.

Our thoughts, too, depend on others. Consider how our minds are shaped fundamentally by the cultures into which we are born and the languages that we acquire through interactions with others. A person's worldview, for example, is powerfully influenced by the beliefs of one's primary caretakers. We can formulate thoughts in part because we have learned languages by which thoughts can be conceived and expressed, and we have acquired those languages from others. Imagine a person alone on an island, with no human connection or interaction from birth until death. What thoughts could such a person think? With no knowledge of mathematics or logic or nutrition, and with no language by which to formulate cogent and nuanced ideas, consider how different such a person would be from anyone else in the world. The extent of that enormous difference illustrates the extent to which our entire cognitive experience depends upon other people.

Our emotional experience involves others to the same degree. Think about how much your day depends on the thoughts and feelings you are having about others—a difficult boss, a threatening coworker, a challenging teenager, or a critical or wonderful partner. Even when alone, we have thoughts and feelings about our interactions with others that color the ways we experience every moment. Love, hate, frustration, happiness, irritation, sorrow, joy—all are emotional expressions of our experiences with other people.

Everything we have said about others' influence on us applies as well to our influence on others. Friedrich Nietzsche famously said that "a 'thing' is the sum of its effects." A person's impact travels way beyond his or her physical body. Voices travel. Communications touch minds. Emotions move hearts. The influences we have on others send ripples across the world. Humankind mingles together almost on the wind, individual and collective human impact reverberating through homes, companies, communities, and nations.

If there is one truism about life, surely it is that we are inextricably and inescapably *together*. The story of how Western thought developed to a point where it seems to contradict the inherently connected lives that we live is a story of man-made boundaries and imagined separations that split mankind from the world, from each other, and finally even from oneself. It is a nihilistic path, and many modern self-help and leadership theories walk it.

Incredibly, a large percentage of people today can quote the starting point of Descartes's four hundred-year-old philosophical work: "I think, therefore I am." This short sentence may seem benign, but Descartes's statement positioned the isolated human self as the fundamental unit of existence. Over time, a number of philosophers began to question this assumption. Hegel, Kierkegaard, Nietzsche, Heidegger, and Buber, among others, started to undercut the logic of the individualistic separations inherent in modern thought. Given that no one is born into this world without others, that one's ability to think requires language learned from others, and that one's cognitive and emotional experiences are shaped by thoughts and feelings about others, thinkers began to argue that individualistic approaches miss the mark. What is fundamental is not an isolated self but rather a kind of brute fact that just is—the reality of being in the world with others. Who we are is *who we are with others.*

Martin Buber, who studied the reality of humankind's connectedness, observed that there are basically two ways of being with others: we can be in the world seeing others as they are, as people, or we can be in the world seeing others as they are not, as objects. He called the first way of being the *I-You* way and the second the *I-It* way. The hyphen in *I-You* on the one hand and *I-It* on the other means that, contrary to Descartes's view, there is no separate "I" way. We are always in relation, inescapably and reciprocally together, both affecting and being affected by others. We can be connected to others as with people or connected to others as with objects, but we are always connected. Separation is an abstraction. Together is our reality.[1]

Let's pause here to explore why this philosophical history matters, even today. Specifically, let's think about what it means for leadership. Consider two different leaders, one of whom is isolated and inherently distinct from those he or she leads (as many modern approaches imply) and one of whom is not. We will call the first leader the *Isolated Leader* and the second leader the *Together Leader*.

Let's examine the differences between these leaders, illustrated in diagram 4.

The Isolated Leader is an inherently isolated human mind, necessarily apart and disconnected from those he leads. He occupies the position of *subject* in his experience, which makes those he leads *objects* in the world of his experience. Which is to say that the leader experiences himself as inherently separate from those he leads. He is *the leader* and others are *the led*. From his separated stance, the Isolated Leader keeps leader-like opportunities, responsibilities, and benefits to himself. He does this not out of malice but as the logical extension of his worldview: leader-like

DIAGRAM 4. **TWO TYPES OF LEADERS**

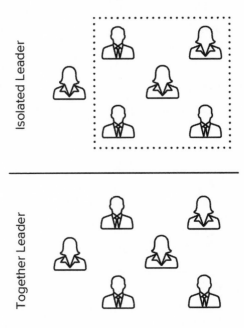

things necessarily attach to the one who is the leader. His responsibilities, obligations, opportunities, and rewards are unique to his leader-self. The Isolated Leader also believes in his own ability to ascertain the truth about the objects on his team. The division between himself and others gives him a vantage point from which to observe and, he believes, comprehend them. Circumscribing them as objects, they seem contained and manageable.

The Together Leader sees an entirely different world. She understands that she occupies the leadership seat at this point in time, but she also realizes that this makes her no different from those she leads. She and her team members are doing something *together*. She realizes that the people she leads are people like herself—that is, subjects in their own right—with boundless possibilities and perspectives. And she understands that her status as a leader actually is granted her by those she would lead. She is not bewitched by her position to think that she has abilities or insights unique to herself. Responsibilities, obligations, opportunities, and rewards are shared in ways that make the most sense for the mission of the team. Since the Together Leader realizes that those she leads are people like herself and are subjects in their own right, she is under no illusion that she can categorize or totalize or mechanically circumscribe them. She lives in the presence of wonder at their thoughts and abilities and therefore provides space for them to create and grow and for her to create and grow in response to them.

With Buber's observations in mind, we can see that both of these leaders are connected with others rather than split from them. It's just that one of them—the Isolated leader—is together with others as with objects, while the Together Leader is together with others as with people. The latter version of leadership is congruent with reality, while the former—the one that presumes the individualism of modern thought—is at war with reality.

It follows from this that in our leadership and general approach to life, we are always either dividing or bringing together—either assuming and wielding splits that don't exist or seeing and valuing the equal humanity in ourselves and others.

As foreshadowed by Martin Buber, which of these we are doing, and the resulting influence we are having on ourselves and others, depends on which of two mindsets we are carrying.

4. TWO MINDSETS

Continuing our discussion from chapter 3, in this chapter we will consider how those who adopt the mindset of a Together Leader are able to find solutions that people operating as Isolated Leaders never can.

Louise Francesconi was president of one of the legacy Howard Hughes companies during a period of consolidation within its industry. The company's chief competitor had recently purchased the company Louise led. After the purchase came a directive: Louise and her executive team had to cut $100 million from the cost side of the business. They were given thirty days. This directive came with an implied "or else." Louise asked us to help them with this challenge.

You can imagine the pressure on Louise and her leadership team. The acquiring company's executives were about to determine their immediate career opportunities. Cutting $100 million was their job interview.

So the members of Louise's team had no choice but to deliver, not just on this group directive, but also in their individual capacities as leaders of separate product lines. Not surprisingly, this created tension within the team. The executives focused on how they each could preserve their own parts of the company, implying that their colleagues should shoulder the bulk of the cost-cutting burden. They did not say this directly to one other, but it became clear as they each briefed the team on what they themselves could do to cut costs. They all offered token cuts in their operational areas, combined with well-prepared arguments for why further cuts would be damaging to the company. To a person, they agreed that the only way to cut $100 million was to lay off a bunch of people. And each of them wanted those layoffs to come primarily from others' parts of the business.

The situation wasn't going anywhere, and Louise grew frustrated. She knew they were going to find $100 million to cut. They had to. But it was going to be painful, and she worried about what that might do to her team and the company going forward.

In our work with organizations, we have seen this kind of impasse many times. At its heart, the problem is pretty simple: incentive structures, company metrics, career goals, and personal egos all conspire to keep people focused on themselves and their own perceived needs and challenges, usually to the detriment of the team and the enterprise. In short, organizations and their people get inwardly focused, and as a result, they get stuck.

Fortunately for Louise and her team, they found a way to get unstuck. Two very important incidents occurred that enabled this to happen. The first was that the group began to consider who would be affected by layoffs if that was the route they decided to go. On a flip chart, these executives began listing those most likely to be affected. As each category of persons was added to the list, the team discussed what layoffs would mean for that group.

Early on, this conversation felt strained. They were talking about people, not because they were inclined to, but because they'd been asked to. But as the list of names and groups grew, they broke into a discussion that began to engage them. They started to really consider those who would be put at risk. *What would this mean for the union? What would this mean for family members of people who might lose their jobs? What would this mean for the community?* As they realized the difficulties that layoffs would present, they gradually became committed to finding alternatives to layoffs where possible.

This was a shift in their shared mindset. It was a shift from seeing themselves as fundamentally separate from others to seeing themselves and others as fundamentally connected. It was an escape from the modern mistake discussed in chapter 3. This led to a second breakthrough. The Arbinger consultant who was working with Louise's team asked the executives to pair up. They were each to spend the next two hours meeting one-on-one with two or three of their colleagues. The assignment was twofold. First, they were asked to learn as much as they could about one another's areas of the business. Second, over the course of this sharing, each was to think about what he or she could do to help the other preserve the vital parts of his or her segments of the business. The task was not to help their colleagues to *cut* their budgets but rather to identify what they each could do to help the colleagues *save*—that is, *preserve*—their budgets.

Asking people to figure out what they could do to keep their colleagues from having to cut money might seem an odd way to cut $100 million. However, surprising things started to happen during these one-on-one meetings. As colleagues learned more about their team members' respective parts of the business, they found themselves *wanting* to help their colleagues with their challenges. They began offering to make some cuts in their own areas of the business to preserve key parts of their colleagues' areas.

As one of Louise's executives learned more about the work of his colleague, he started to wonder if it wouldn't make good business sense, and save a great deal of money, if he folded his own division into his colleague's. Consider what this meant: a leader who reported directly to the president of the company was considering stepping down a level and reporting to someone who, up to that moment, was his peer. He shared this idea aloud.

Like SWAT team members mixing baby bottles, this is the sort of thing that doesn't happen very often. The reason it doesn't is because people can't consider such a move from the perspective of the kind of mindset that normally prevails in organizations — especially in pressure-filled situations like the one Louise and her team were in.

This single move, where one executive folded his portion of the business beneath one of his colleagues, saved the company $7 million. This was the first of a number of collaborative steps that enabled them to cut the full $100 million while improving rather than harming the organization. A challenge that had the potential to divide the team or result in indiscriminate cuts that could have damaged the business over the longer term ended up becoming the impetus for innovative thinking that made the business healthier and better.

The way Louise and her team came together to meet the challenge of cutting $100 million became their mode of working together. They began collaborating this way year after year. Early on, the members of her executive team needed a full day to collaboratively set the annual goals for their highly complex organization. After a couple of years, they were able to pull this off in half a day. Ultimately, they found they could complete the process in an hour, as the annual goal-setting work became simply an extension of the way they worked together on a daily basis.

Over this period, they doubled the business at a time experts thought it couldn't grow more than 5 percent.

Let's examine some key differences between the way Louise's team initially tried to tackle the challenge of cutting $100 million and how they later were able to accomplish their goal. Diagram 5 shows these differences.

DIAGRAM 5. **LOUISE'S TEAM**

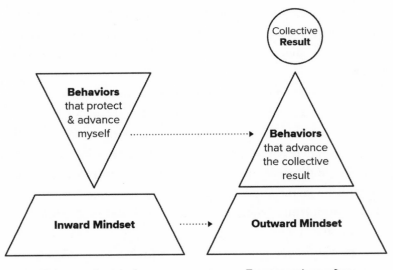

The team had a collective target result. They needed to cut $100 million in costs. In the beginning, they were understandably concerned about their own futures with the company. All were strongly motivated to preserve their own positions and status in the organization. With this mindset, they could consider only those options that would advance their own agendas. We illustrate this by pointing the behavior triangle at the person. We call this way of operating an *inward mindset*.

When they broke free from the constraints of self-concern, the team members were able to consider options that hadn't occurred to them when their mindsets were inward. As they focused together on the collective result, their mindsets turned *outward*. We illustrate this by pointing the behavior triangle at the collective result.

Notice how people think about and do different things depending on their mindset. With an inward mindset, people behave in ways that are calculated to benefit themselves. With an outward mindset, people are able to consider and behave in ways that further the collective results that they are committed to achieve.

These two mindsets—an inward mindset on the one hand and an outward mindset on the other—form two ends of a continuum, as illustrated in diagram 6. Consider, for example, an organization in which every person operates with an inward mindset and where the practices, policies, and processes continually invite the same. No organization is completely this way, but consider this extreme case as the left end of the mindset continuum. Then consider an organization composed of people, processes, and practices that are entirely outward. Again, no single organization operates with a completely outward mindset, but consider that possibility as the extreme right end of the continuum.

In our work, we both assess and invite clients to self-assess where they are on this continuum. We do this to get a baseline against which to measure progress. It is interesting to see how people rate their own organizations. If an entirely inward mindset is 0 on the scale and an entirely outward mindset is 10, a relatively small percentage of groups assess their own organizations

DIAGRAM 6. **THE MINDSET CONTINUUM**

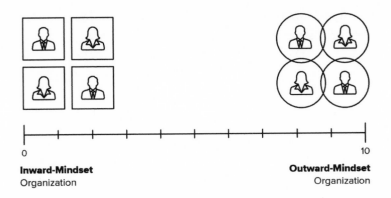

0	10
Inward-Mindset	**Outward-Mindset**
Organization	Organization

at higher than 5 on this continuum, with most rating them at somewhere between 2 and 4.

It probably won't surprise you that people almost universally rate themselves much higher (i.e., as more outward) on this continuum than they rate their colleagues and organizations. This is corroborated by results of a mindset assessment we use with companies. When we average the results across industries, people rate their colleagues at 4.6 on the continuum and themselves at 6.8. Think about what this means: on average, all employees in an organization think they are nearly 50 percent better—more collaborative and less blameworthy—than their coworkers. So what happens when problems arise? Those who think they are 7s look around and wait for all the 4s to change. The trouble is, all those 4s think they, too, are 7s! So everyone waits—and blames. This is a manifestation of the problem of self-deception that we wrote about in *Leadership and Self-Deception.*

Whatever the scores are, the objective is to move individuals and organizations further to the right on the mindset continuum.

Why? Because accountability, collaboration, innovation, leadership, culture, and value to customers all improve as organizations increasingly apply an outward mindset in their strategies, structures, systems, processes, and day-to-day work.

5. SEEING TRUTHFULLY

In chapter 4, we introduced the inward and outward mindsets and saw both at work in Louise Francesconi's executive team. Their shift from an inward to an outward mindset illustrates how people are able to consider better possibilities when their mindsets are outward because they see beyond themselves and can think beyond narrow self-interest.

A shift to an outward mindset also changes how people see, regard, and engage with others. We saw this, too, in the experience of Louise's team. As their mindsets turned outward, they began to see and consider not only their own needs but also the needs and objectives of others—the needs of their colleagues and of those who might be affected by potential layoffs. Breakthroughs came as they began considering others in this way. Seeing others differently, they began thinking and behaving differently.

Beginning in this chapter, we will get much more specific about the differences between outward and inward mindsets. Let's begin by considering the outward mindset.

A person whose mindset is outward sees others as people. Seeing them as people, he realizes that others matter like he himself matters. And because they do, their needs, objectives, and challenges will matter to him as well. As a result, his objectives and behaviors will take others into account. In a work context, a person with an outward mindset will hold himself accountable to accomplish his own objectives and to do so in a way that makes it easier, not harder, for his colleagues to succeed in their responsibilities as well.

By contrast, a person whose mindset is inward sees others more like objects—like vehicles to use, for example, obstacles to blame, or irrelevancies to ignore. From his point of view, others don't really matter like he matters. He is consumed with his own objectives, and the needs, objectives, and challenges of others don't really matter to him. His own objectives and behaviors become self-focused. On the job, such a person may successfully achieve his objectives, but he won't care if the way he does his work makes it harder for others to achieve theirs.

One way to summarize the difference between outward and inward mindsets is in terms of accountability: At best, someone with an inward mindset holds himself accountable for his own actions and performance. At worst, he blames his poor performance on others. Either way, he sees and experiences himself in an isolated, separated way. This alone doesn't mean he is a bad person. It just means that his focus has gotten narrow in a way that blinds him to some of what is going on around him. In contrast, someone with an outward mindset holds himself accountable both for his own actions and performance and for his impact on others' actions and performance. He understands that he is connected with others and holds himself accountable for the impact of his manner of connection. He can see.

We illustrate a few of these key differences in diagrams 7 and 8. A person whose mindset is outward sees others as *people*, so their needs, objectives, and challenges matter to him. The triangle on the outward-mindset diagram is turned outward to signify how, when one is seeing others as people, one's objectives and behaviors take others into account.

DIAGRAM 7. **THE OUTWARD MINDSET AND OTHERS**

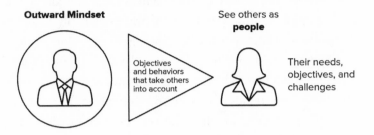

DIAGRAM 8. **THE INWARD MINDSET AND OTHERS**

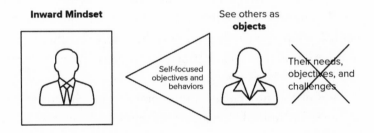

In contrast, a person whose mindset is inward sees others as objects, so their needs, objectives, and challenges don't really matter. The triangle on the inward-mindset diagram is turned inward to signify the self-focused nature of the objectives and behaviors of one whose mindset is inward.

The words *outward* and *inward* are helpful terms for capturing the core idea of an others-inclusive way of seeing and engaging with people as opposed to a self-centered way of seeing and engaging with people. However, the terms can create misunderstanding in a couple of ways. First of all, we are not speaking of personality types, such as extroverted and introverted people.

Extroverts can be very self-focused and therefore inward, just as introverts can be very good at seeing others and taking them into account. Outward and inward mindsets apply to both of these and any other personality types. Secondly, don't confuse introspection with an inward mindset. One can introspect in a self-centered way, which *would* indicate an inward mindset. However, a person also can introspect about one's connections with others as well, which is the very essence of what we are calling *outwardness*. Sometimes it is helpful to look *inside* to see how one is connected with what is *outside*.

This kind of outward-mindset introspection is a strategic imperative for the healthcare company that we discussed in chapter 1. Its success is directly tied to how the employees of that company purposely reflect on how they are with others, trying to become aware of and interested in the needs, objectives, and challenges of their coworkers and customers.

One of the first facilities the company purchased had experienced perennial struggles, both clinically and financially. The facility was led by an interdisciplinary team of talented department heads who had, over time, forgotten the reason they entered healthcare. Years of inwardly focused management had invited and reinforced an inward focus in them, often leaving them blind to their impact on each other and, most importantly, the patients in their care. During the first few months after the acquisition of this facility, an elderly Vietnamese patient was admitted from the local hospital.

While traveling back to Vietnam after visiting her children in another location in the United States, this patient had experienced major health complications. Unable to speak English and with no family nearby, she was powerless to communicate with the staff at even the most basic levels and quickly became a problem. One behavioral outburst followed another—first she threw her food and then her urinal—each eruption accompanied by yells and rants in a language none of the staff understood. "She has to be discharged," one department leader demanded in the next department-head meeting. "Surely there is a behavioral unit that will accept her." Another agreed: "At the very least, we have to get the physician to prescribe medication to calm her down."

With these two options on the table, the team stood to leave the meeting. "What would it be like to be her?" one of the team members asked quietly, almost to herself, giving voice to an outward-mindset question. Everyone stopped. "I'm just thinking about what it would be like to be Ms. Tham," she continued. "She is far from home. She can't communicate. She can't understand what is going on. She doesn't know why we are keeping her here or if she'll ever get home. I wonder what she's thinking? What would that be like?"

Everyone sat down again. After a few moments, the dietary supervisor spoke up: "You know, there is a little Vietnamese store by my house. Maybe it would make a difference if she could eat what she's used to eating. I'll get some recipes online and see what we could do in the kitchen." The social services director began searching for local Vietnamese community groups and within the week had a lineup of volunteers to be at Ms. Tham's bedside spending one-on-one time in conversation and providing translation services for the nurses. Soon the entire staff had rallied to find ways not only to make Ms. Tham's stay bearable but to enrich it. She was no longer an object to the people in the facility; she had become a person to them—a person whom they desired to help.

Notice how the team members exercised their best thinking when they began to see and consider Ms. Tham as a person. The same could be said of Chip's squad members and Louise's executive team. Seeing people as people rather than as objects enables better thinking because such thinking is done in response to the truth: others really are people and not objects.

This truth, once seen, enables change even where change seems most unlikely. For example, consider the story of Ivan Cornia and his father, William.

Ivan was born in 1929. During the years of the Great Depression, his father sandwiched long days manning the local canal between morning and evening work on the family farm. William's boss on his day job was a very difficult man, and William often returned home from his shift in an angry mood. He tried to find refuge in the bottle, and the mixture of anger and alcohol drove him to violence, starting with the animals on the family farm. For example, on one occasion when reshoeing one of his horses, the horse jerked its foot and ripped William's leg open. William jumped up, grabbed a metal rasp, and crashed it against the horse's head. Young Ivan was holding the horse by its bridle at the time, and twelve hundred pounds of horseflesh collapsed to the ground at his feet. Ivan thought his father had killed it.

Ivan had witnessed his father beating sheep, cows, goats, and dogs numerous times. He lived in constant fear that he would be next.

One early morning, Ivan and his father were in the barn together. Ivan was milking one of the cows while his father was taking care of other chores. As Ivan milked his cow, the cow in the next stall switched its tail, which was just long enough to reach Ivan.

One of the burrs on the end of the cow's tail caught Ivan in the eye. Without thinking, Ivan leapt up, grabbed the metal milk stool he had been sitting on, and, while shouting the vile obscenities he had heard his father yell, began beating the cow violently. When he had unleashed all his anger, he put the stool back down and collapsed onto it, readying himself to continue milking. But then something horrifying occurred to him: the cow he had just pulverized was his father's favorite cow, and his father was working barely twenty feet behind him. Ivan began quivering and sunk lower on his stool. He buried his head into the flank of the cow and waited, heart pounding, sure that the time for his beating had come.

But his father didn't come. Besides Ivan's heavy breathing, the barn lay shrouded in silence.

After what seemed like an eternity, Ivan's father quietly approached and placed a stool next to his son. Then he heard his father softly say, "Ivan, if you'll stop, I'll stop."

Recalling this story some seventy years later, Ivan said that from that moment on he'd never known a more gentle, helpful, and kind human being. William Cornia completely and irrevocably changed his life—all at once. No more violence, no more vile language, no more alcohol. He became a different person in an instant. No one who knew William at the time would have guessed that he could change like this, and certainly not all at once. How was he able to do it?

William found the ability to do what he had previously been unable to do in the moment he saw the needs of his son and realized that he was responsible for his impact on his boy. William's change was dramatic because it was not merely a change in what he did; it was a change in how he *saw* and *thought*.

Rok Zorko, vice president of product development for the very successful app-development company, Outfit7, said, "It is an eye-opener to realize that you are not to treat people as objects but to treat them as people. Once you have this knowledge, you can never unthink it." Evidently, this was true for William Cornia as well. Once he saw the impact he had on his son, he could not unsee it. Seeing Ivan in this way was William's escape from his inward mindset. He ended up raising a son who became a revered art teacher in the public school system and had the same kind of life-changing impact on countless students.

William, Louise and her executive team, Chip and his SWAT squad, and the healthcare workers with Ms. Tham were able to move to an outward mindset when they saw beyond themselves and discovered the needs of those around them. Through the rest of this book, we will consider many additional real-life examples to further explore the differences in the inward and outward mindsets and to help illuminate how to live and work more consistently with an outward mindset.

In part II, we explore the inward and outward mindsets in more depth and consider the consequences of each mindset both personally and organizationally. We detail the outward-mindset pattern, a step-by-step blueprint that, if implemented, enables a person or organization to consistently operate with an outward mindset. In part III, we present important issues to consider and helpful strategies that individuals and organizations can implement to help teams and entire organizations turn outward.

PART II
TURNING MINDSET OUTWARD

6.   GETTING OUT OF OUR OWN WAY

For all the advantages that an outward mindset seems to offer, why would people ever be inward? It is tempting to blame difficult circumstances or challenging people. However, in our experience, what keeps people from an outward mindset is themselves. We get in our own way.

You might find yourself in circumstances that make this claim sound naive. Your boss may be difficult to work for. Perhaps you feel beat down by a critical spouse or overwhelmed by challenging children. You might be on the brink of financial ruin or feel as if your career has hit a dead end. In response to these or other difficulties, perhaps you have felt compelled toward an inward mindset. If so, we understand. We've been there too.

But we've also been privileged to know people who, despite their own challenges, have been able to find their way to an outward mindset. And we've seen how much better off they are for having done so. One such person is Chris Wallace. A seventeen-year-old girl taught him that his mindset was his choice, no matter the difficulty of his challenges. We are grateful to Chris for allowing us to share his story. Although deeply personal, its lessons apply everywhere and, we believe, to everyone.

On a sweltering August day in 1967, then sixteen-year-old Chris was cutting hay on his family's ranch. Named by his father after Chris's mother, Margaret, the Santa Margarita Ranch was a magnificent thirty-nine-hundred-acre spread located one hundred miles southeast of Reno, Nevada. A river flowed through the middle of the ranch, lined by cottonwood and poplar trees that made it an inviting getaway from both the monotonous hard work of the ranch and the heat of the summer Nevada sun. On this day, Chris was operating the swather, a machine that cuts hay and funnels the cuttings into narrow swaths, or windrows. He was on the seat of the swather grousing to himself about his father.

His father, Nate Wallace, had been raised on a wheat farm in Northern California where he was one of the first crop-duster pilots in the state. He and Margaret married soon after meeting in Carson City, Nevada. Together, they acquired and ran a private airport in Reno. They sold the airport a few years later for a huge profit and plowed the revenues into three ranches, which they assembled into the Santa Margarita Ranch. It was Nate's way of returning to his roots. For Chris and the rest of the children, the ranch was both a symbol of social status and the source of a dreary string of endless obligations.

When Chris was fourteen, his way of escape from the ranch presented itself in the person of his wealthy uncle Dick, visiting from Pennsylvania. "I'd like to take Chris back with me to introduce him to the East—the cities, the museums, the civil war sites, his cousins—and show him what is possible in business," he said to Chris's father while at the dinner table one night. The business he mentioned happened to be one of Nelson Rockefeller's companies. Chris's uncle was then president of the company. "I think it will prepare Chris for big things," Uncle Dick said.

Chris was stunned by this pronouncement. He had grown up with stories of the wealth and success of his mother's family but had never been back East to see it for himself. He could hardly contain his excitement as he pictured life away from the dusty roads and endless fields of the Santa Margarita Ranch. He turned and looked hopefully at his father.

Nate wiped his mouth with his napkin as he finished chewing a mouthful of pot roast. He shook his head. "That's a generous offer, Dick," he said, "but it's not something we'll be able to do." Chris's spirit, which a moment before had been soaring, slammed headlong into the dusty high-desert reality that suddenly seemed both a ceiling and a prison. Chris silently looked down at his plate of food and felt resentment toward his father swell within him.

Chris's anger simmered to the point that he got up abruptly and ran from the house. His father came out looking for him, but Chris wanted nothing to do with him and remained stealthily silent. In his mind, his father had just sentenced him to a life that he suddenly hated. He hid on the pump-house roof until long after his father had given up the search.

Chris replayed the memory of that evening in his mind as he finished cutting the alfalfa for the day. Over the intervening two years, he had grown distant from his father. He performed his required daily chores but offered no more of himself than that— no words, no extra effort, no understanding or gratitude. Upon finishing his basic daily responsibilities, he would disappear into the brush along the river, trying to escape his life by losing himself in books that he borrowed from his father's library.

Although Chris wasn't paying attention to it, the family's financial situation had grown precarious. Uncle Dick offered to take care of their crushing load of debt, but Chris's father flatly refused the help. Instead, at the end of his rope, he agreed to deed the massive Santa Margarita Ranch to a neighbor in a humiliating exchange for a small 160-acre ranch and a local nine-hole golf course. The imminent loss of the ranch made Chris feel as if they were just country-bumpkin losers. To Chris, it was one more reason to hate his father.

As Chris neared the house this particular evening, he heard his parents quarreling. He had never heard them argue before. Chris opened the door just in time to see his father strike his mother with his hand—a sight much more shocking to Chris than the sound of their quarreling. The righteous indignation Chris felt on behalf of his mother acted like a spark to the two years' worth of combustible resentment that bubbled within him. He sprinted into his parents' bedroom and grabbed his father's pistol. Wild-eyed and livid, he chased his father out of the house.

On a night just two months later, Chris's life was changed forever. After retiring to bed, he was awakened by two loud noises— the first the firing of a gun and the second the thud of a body hitting the floor. He awoke to discover that his father had killed himself with the same gun Chris had wielded against him.

Chris's older brother ran into Chris's bedroom to tell him what had just happened, but Chris had no desire to go in his parents' bedroom to see the scene. From the hallway, he could see his father's foot. That was enough for Chris. He felt free now that his father was dead.

Nate Wallace's death put tremendous strain on the family at a time when they were already experiencing terrible hardship. Chris blamed his father for all of it—for their economic misfortune, for leaving Chris's mother to handle everything, and for embarrassing the family and making them feel like social outcasts. Chris became consumed with anger.

When anything went wrong in his life, he blamed his father for it. A failed relationship? His father's fault. Difficulty in a class at school? Also his father's fault. Indecision about his future? What would you expect from one who had no father to advise and counsel him?

When Chris lay down at night, his father ruined even his sleep. Frequently Chris dreamed of seeing his father outside a building or across a parking lot or field. But by the time Chris reached the spot where his father had been, he had disappeared. Night after night Chris relived this scenario, his father still abandoning him.

Chris had learned that he could garner great sympathy by telling others about his father's suicide and how his father still haunted his dreams. The beginning of Chris's lessons in mind-set change happened on an evening when Chris, who was twenty-one at the time, told his story to a seventeen-year-old girl we'll call Ann. Unlike others he'd told the story to, she wasn't buying it. Upon hearing Chris's story, she started chuckling.

"Why are you laughing?" Chris asked angrily.

Ann didn't respond immediately.

"There's nothing funny about it," Chris stammered. "Why do you laugh?"

"Well," she responded, "your dad is dead, right?"

Chris just looked at her.

"So those things going on inside your head—he's not responsible for them; *you* are. They're *your* dreams."

That thought had never occurred to Chris before. He puzzled over it.

Ann continued: "If you could catch up to him, what would you tell him?"

"I'd tell him all the things he did wrong," Chris answered, getting worked up. "I'd tell him off—about how he'd hurt Mom and hurt us."

Ann scratched her head for a moment. "That's interesting. In your sleep, you can't allow yourself to confront your father. It must be because, at some level, you don't want to add to his pain."

This thought came from so far afield that Chris could hardly process it. It had never occurred to him until that moment that his father had burdens. Chris had only been alive to his own.

"So what *should* I tell him, then?" he challenged her.

"I don't know," she responded. "Maybe you could apologize for hating and resenting him all these years."

Chris exploded: "Look, if anyone should apologize, it's him! He ruined my life."

"No, Chris," she said. "He ruined *his* life. You're ruining yours."

Chris couldn't even speak in response to this. He wandered away in a stupor.

Chris kept thinking about what Ann had said to him, and for three weeks, his father didn't show up in his dreams. Then, one dream-filled night, Chris saw his father walking down the opposite side of a street. When Chris saw him, his father ducked into a hardware store. Chris quickly crossed the street and entered the store himself. Instead of finding the store empty, which had been what happened in every such dream before, on this night, Chris entered to find his father standing just four feet in front of him. After all these years, Chris was face-to-face with his dad.

What would he tell him?

The dreaming version of Chris took young Ann's advice. He offered his apology and he and his father fell into an embrace.

When Chris awakened, he found himself filled with an entirely new sensation: *he missed his father.* All the acrimony he had been carrying was replaced by longing.

This longing for his father is a feeling that more than forty-four years later has never left Chris. When he thinks about this personal metamorphosis, he draws a powerful conclusion from it. "We're so convinced that how we think and feel about other people is caused by *them*," he says, "by what they have or haven't done, by how inconsiderate they have been to us or how judgmental, and so on. But a seventeen-year-old young woman taught me that this wasn't true. I see people the way I see them because of *me*."

When questioned whether he isn't just giving his father a pass for the hardship he caused, Chris doesn't flinch. "No, I just stopped giving myself a pass. That didn't mean I started giving my dad one. I can see his failings. He made some mistakes, including one particularly horrible, terrible mistake—one I bet he would have wanted to take back the moment after he did it, had that mistake not ended his ability to do so. But I don't dwell on his mistakes anymore, the way I used to fixate on his failings as a way of denying my own."

When questioned what mistakes Chris had made of his own, he starts to tear up. "I didn't really see my dad back then. Not really. I took him for granted. All I really cared about was what I wanted to be doing. I never tried to appreciate the heavy burdens that he shouldered—the huge debt and needs of a large family. I guess as a teenager there were limits to what I could have understood, but the point is that I didn't even try. Not even a little.

"Had I tried," he continued, "I might have been able to consider how my father wasn't trying to ruin my future when he told Uncle Dick that I couldn't go back East with him but that he and my family needed me. In fact, it's possible that my father didn't want me to go partly because he didn't want to miss out on my final growing-up years. Who can just up and wave goodbye to their youngest child when he is just fourteen? I know I couldn't. And neither could he."

Chris shakes his head at the thought. "I raged at my dad for not caring, when it's far more likely that he did what he did because he cared so much. But I didn't see it. I never gave my father a chance to explain. I wasn't interested in an alternative to my explanation for why he said what he did. Instead, I just turned away from him and retreated into myself.

"So you ask what mistakes I made?" Chris repeats the question, looking the questioner straight in the eyes. "I made the mistake of just focusing on myself, which made me miss and misinterpret so much that was around me. I wonder every day if things in the family wouldn't have gone differently had I just tried to see."

As we discussed in chapter 5, this interest in the needs and objectives of others is what sets the outward-mindset individual apart from those who are burdened with an inward mindset. When my mindset is outward, I am alive to and interested in other people and their objectives and needs. I see others as people whom I am open to helping. When my mindset is inward, on the other hand, I essentially turn my back on others; I don't really care about their needs or objectives.

Not caring in this way might seem to make my life simpler, but nothing could be further from the truth. Not caring to notice or be moved by others requires something of me that takes a tremendous personal and social toll: it requires me to feel justified for not caring.

I find justification by focusing on others' faults, real and imagined. I take up a self-justifying and others-blaming narrative, which comes at great personal and social cost. I value other people's failures because they give me an excuse for why I shouldn't have to help them, and I value my own personal failures, as Chris did his, because they give me proof that others have done me wrong.[1]

Let's consider how this happens. Think about the following situation. Let's say that I work with someone named Lori. Suppose that one day I come across a piece of information that will be very helpful to me in my work. Suppose as well that from my understanding of Lori's needs and objectives, I realize that the information would be very helpful to Lori. If I have an outward mindset, knowing that the organization's success depends on my colleague's success as well as my own, I will feel an obligation to help my colleague succeed. Recognizing that Lori would be helped by the information, I will have the desire to share it with her.

But I don't have to. I still have a choice. What if I were to choose *not* to share the information? What do you suppose might happen to my mindset?

What if Lori once did something that made a situation harder for me? As I begin to entertain the possibility of not sharing the information with her, do you think that I might remember that time when she didn't help me? What if she has some annoying habits? Do you think I might start thinking about how annoying she can be?

Maybe I don't know Lori very well. Not knowing her would give me a lot of room to imagine what she must *really* be like. What picture of Lori would make it easier for me to feel justified for not sharing the information? Lori as hardworking or lazy? Trustworthy or unreliable? Helpful or uncooperative?

With an inward mindset, I see Lori in distorted ways—ways that help me feel justified for deciding not to help her. I will zero in on anything about her or the situation that will give me this apparent justification. *She doesn't help me,* I might say to myself. *And she's really an annoying person. You can't trust her either; no one who is really trustworthy has such shifty eyes. Besides, if she worked harder, she would've discovered the information herself. I shouldn't reward slothfulness. No, that wouldn't be good for the company. It would really be a mistake if I shared this with her.* My self-talk and how I am now feeling toward Lori will justify the way I am choosing to live.

This is similar to the way Chris was seeing his father. From Chris's inward-mindset perspective, his father was to blame for everything that had gone wrong in Chris's life. Chris felt he was doing the best he could do under the circumstances.

Chris's mindset began changing when he started to shift his focus from his own troubles to the troubles of his father. This was no easy feat in his situation. But eventually he was able to turn some of his attention to his father—not to blame him but to understand him. This willingness unlocked Chris from the dark and cramped space where he had been confining himself to live.

Consider your own situations. For years Chris resisted the needs, burdens, and challenges of his father. Are there people in your life, either at work or at home, whose needs, objectives, and burdens *you* resist seeing? How about people that you *don't* resist—people with whom you are open, curious, interested, aware?

As you compare these relationships, what differences do you notice in how you feel and act? Can you spot any blame in what you tell yourself about others or any self-justifying narratives that you've come to believe about yourself? In which relationships do you notice these blaming, self-justifying narratives? The ones in which you are alive to and interested in the needs, objectives, and challenges of others or the ones in which you are not?

Chris's experience suggests that the most troubling areas of our lives will be those in which we resist what the humanity of others invites us to see. This is a hopeful truth. It means that, like Chris, we can be rid of the distorted ways of seeing that strain our connections with others. We can stop resisting.

7. THE LURE OF INWARDNESS

In the prior chapter, we discussed how people who choose to dismiss the needs and objectives of others end up searching for ways to justify that choice. Within organizations, every person who is burning time and energy seeking justification is doing so at the expense of the contribution he or she could be making to the overall results of the company. The energy-draining, time-wasting, silo-creating effect of this justification seeking is one of the most debilitating of organizational problems.

Diagram 9 illustrates the inward mindset that is at the root of these workplace issues.

DIAGRAM 9. **THE INWARD MINDSET AT WORK**

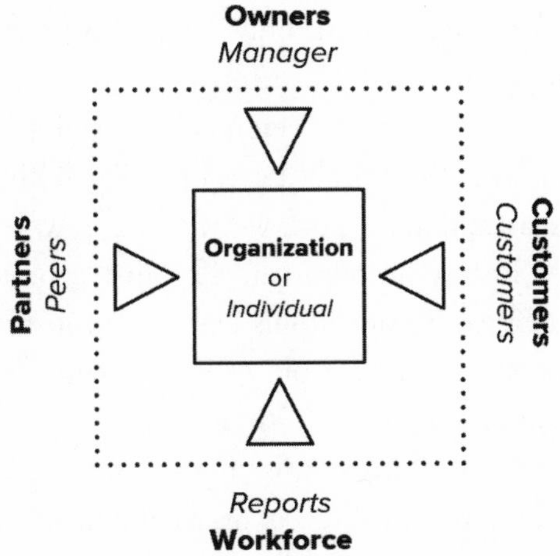

Owners
Manager

Partners
Peers

Organization
or
Individual

Customers
Customers

Reports
Workforce

Often people exhibit an inward mindset toward some people and an outward mindset toward others, but for simplicity, this diagram depicts an organization or individual that is operating with an inward mindset in each of the four basic directions of their work. (The same diagram can be used in other contexts, such as in your personal life, by substituting different categories of people or by adding the names of key people in your life.)

With an inward mindset, a person focuses on what he needs from others to achieve his objectives—what he needs from his customers, direct reports, peers, and leaders or from his children, partner, or neighbor. He is primarily concerned with others' impact on him rather than with his impact on them. We capture these realities in this diagram by omitting the needs, objectives, and challenges of others and by pointing the triangles inward. Because people plagued with an inward mindset are ignoring the needs, objectives, and challenges of others, they will see their circumstances and execute their work in ways that justify their self-focus.

But *individuals* are not the only ones who find themselves stuck in an inward mindset. *Entire organizations* can fall prey to the lure of inwardness with spectacularly damaging results.

To illustrate what this mindset can look like, both at the individual and organizational levels, we will share two experiences from our own history at Arbinger. The first experience is an example of how easily individuals can succumb to an inward focus. The second is an example of how organizations can be inwardly oriented.

Years ago, when Arbinger was in its early stages as an organization and few people knew of us, we put hundreds of hours of work into a proposal for a large culture-change initiative. On the afternoon we sent the proposal to the prospective client, we looked at each other, wondering what to do next. One of us said, "I can't think of anything. Let's go swimming." And so we swam. And hoped.

A couple of weeks later, we received word that we had been selected as one of the three finalists for the project. The two other finalists were at that time two of the most well-known training and consulting firms in the world. The client informed us that each of the three finalists would have two hours to present its approach to the committee that would be picking the winner. We heard through the grapevine that the company's vice president of human resources had said that he was fine with either of the two well-known companies, but he didn't want to be responsible for bringing in a complete unknown and then having the project fail; he couldn't risk that exposure. So we had a sense of what we were up against.

As we were in the green room waiting to go on, our stomachs were in knots. We were feeling what golf great and world-class character Lee Trevino described when he said, "Putts get real difficult the day they hand out the money," which is to say that we were worrying about ourselves. We were worrying about ourselves because we were seeing the customer relationship backward. We were nervous because we needed the company's money, and we were afraid that if we didn't nail this presentation, the committee wouldn't give us any. The objective in our minds was our own, not our customer's. We were about to present an outward-mindset approach to company-wide culture change while our mindsets were inward.

Thankfully, someone in our group recognized what was going on, and he called us on it. "Hey," he said, "we, of all people, should know better than this. We don't know whether we will get this contract; that's out of our hands anyway. What we do know, however, is that we have two hours to be with these fifteen people. This might be the only time we ever get to spend with them and with this company. What if we just stay focused on being as helpful to them as we can be during these two hours?"

This saved us from ourselves, and as it turned out, we ended up winning the contract. In retrospect, winning this contract probably was essential to Arbinger's survival in the early days of our existence. The irony is that our company benefited only when we took our minds off of our company benefiting. Had we continued with an inward mindset, we would have helped neither the client nor ourselves.

Over the years, we have worked hard as a company to re-member the question that our experience in that green room invited us to ask: Whose needs and objectives—our cus-tomer's or our own—will be our primary focus and concern? Notwithstanding this, many years later we discovered a way in which we had unwittingly adopted an inward mindset around a key portion of our business.

Part of our work is preparing people within our client orga-nizations to be able to facilitate our workshops and implement outward-mindset strategies in their workplaces. We have always really enjoyed training and preparing these internal partners, and we had long believed that we were doing a good job in this part of our business.

But we noticed something that caused us to question our belief about ourselves. We realized that although we were train-ing and preparing many internal experts, our work with them consisted only of helping them become proficient in what we do. Helping them become proficient is important, of course; we needed to continue to do that. But we noticed that we had largely been ignoring something that was of even greater importance. We had not been sufficiently learning about the needs, objectives, and challenges of the organizations that employed them. Because we hadn't been making enough of an effort to understand what these client organizations wanted their internal experts to help them with, we had no way to know if we were really helping. High customer satisfaction scores from our internal partners weren't enough to tell us whether our work was hitting the mark for these organizations.

As on that day many years ago in the green room, we had become blind to how organizationally we had turned inward—obsessing primarily over the quality of our own work rather than over the value our clients were receiving from our work. This reawakening caused us to question a lot of the work we were doing. It caused us to reinvent large portions of our business—how we were structured, where we were spending our time and resources, our client engagement process, and the services we were providing, as well as our success metrics and company goals. We have become our own client in the sense that we use the ideas we share with others to look for the inwardness in ourselves that can so easily sneak into and corrupt individual and organizational efforts.

One of the reasons that we had missed our own inward-mindedness was because as an organization we had taken on an inward-mindset style that can easily be mistaken for an outward mindset. Diagram 10 captures this "outwardly nice" inward-mindset style as it is manifested in both individuals and organizations.

DIAGRAM 10. **THE "OUTWARDLY NICE" INWARD-MINDSET STYLE**

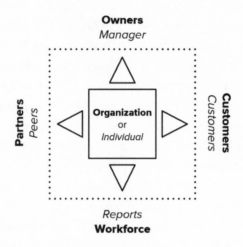

Notice that the triangles in this diagram are turned outward, as they are in the outward-mindset diagram (diagram 7). In contrast to the outward-mindset diagram, however, diagram 10 omits the needs, objectives, and challenges of others. Even though people or organizations operating with this style of inwardness feel as if they are doing things for others and not for themselves, they aren't paying attention to the needs, objectives, and challenges of those they are supposedly doing things for. This raises the following question: If they aren't alive to and interested in the needs, objectives, and challenges of those they are doing things for, for whom are they really doing them?

This is a question we at Arbinger had to ask ourselves. In a way, we found ourselves back in the green room again, facing the same question: *Whose needs and objectives—our customer's or our own—will be our primary focus and concern?*

We have learned through our work with clients that this version of the inward-mindset diagram captures how people and organizations that are inward often experience themselves. They don't experience themselves as being egocentric in the way the standard inward-mindset-at-work diagram (diagram 9) suggests, with the triangles pointed inward. They feel as if they do good things for others all the time and actually experience themselves as being outwardly facing. They experience themselves the way one of our colleagues, Joe Bartley, experienced himself until one of his daughters awakened him to the truth.

Joe was tucking his daughters into bed one evening. After tucking in Sarah, age four, he turned to tuck in Anna, age six. Anna was in a fetal position, facing away from Joe and toward the wall. Joe leaned over her to tuck in her covers. He finished and was about to turn and leave to go help his son, Jacob, with his homework when he heard Anna whisper something. He couldn't tell what she said, but she had definitely whispered something to him. "What was that, Anna?" Joe asked. He bent over to listen.

"You don't love me like you love Jacob," Anna repeated, her voice barely audible.

Joe was momentarily stunned by the comment. He instantly could tell that Anna was really hurting. "Sure I do," he assured her.

"No you don't," she whispered back.

Joe paused for a moment. "Why do you say that?" he finally asked.

Anna still hadn't moved. "You don't play with me like you play with Jacob."

"Sure I do," Joe defended himself. "Every night after I get home from work, we all go out back and play basketball together."

"I don't like basketball," Anna whispered.

To this day, Joe reflects often on this experience. "What kind of a father had I been," he wonders, "that I didn't even know that my little girl didn't like basketball? The truth was that I liked playing basketball, and I counted doing it with my kids as good parenting on my part. But Anna helped me see that I wasn't really seeing my kids. Not really. I was doing what *I* wanted to do with them; I wasn't paying attention to what *they* wanted to do. I was an outwardly nice—even fun-loving—inward-mindset father."

This trap is easy to fall into, especially for those whose roles keep them doing things for others—people in healthcare and hospitality, for example, or educators, counselors, primary caregivers in the home, and so on.

What is the cost of an inward mindset? When people focus on themselves rather than on their impact, lots of activity and effort get wasted on the wrong things. The absence of collaboration results in low levels of innovation. And employees disengage due to the boredom inherent with inward-mindset thinking and working.

In the next chapter, we discuss an outward-mindset way of approaching one's work that can keep people out of these and myriad other problems that are the unavoidable result of an inward mindset.

8. THE OUTWARD-MINDSET SOLUTION

Think about the times in your life when you have felt most alive and engaged. Who and what were you focused on in those moments—on yourself or on something bigger that included others?

Captain Rob Newson, a career Navy SEAL and longtime leader in the Special Operations community, provided an interesting insight on this question when he described the difference between those who successfully complete SEAL qualification training and those who don't. SEAL candidates can quit whenever they want by ringing a bell that hangs at the side of their training area. "I can say with certainty," Captain Newson says, "when those who quit took the first steps toward the bell: the moment they stopped thinking about the mission and their teammates and started thinking primarily about themselves. So long as they stay focused on the mission and those around them, they can get through anything. But the moment they start focusing inward and fixating on how cold, wet, and tired they are, it is not a matter of *if* they will ring out but *when*."

Captain Newson's advice to those who wish to successfully complete one of the most difficult training regimens in the world is to focus on the mission and on those around them. His prescription is the outward mindset.

Our organizational clients find it helpful to apply the outward mindset in the four basic directions of work depicted in diagram 11.

DIAGRAM 11. **THE OUTWARD MINDSET AT WORK**

A person conceiving her work in the way illustrated in this diagram is alive to and interested in the needs, objectives, and challenges of each of the persons toward whom she has responsibility—toward her customers, direct reports, peers, and manager. The outwardly facing triangles show that her objectives and behaviors take these people's needs, objectives, and challenges into account. As Captain Newson recommends, her focus is outward on something much larger than herself—on her essential contribution to the overall goals of the organization. And thinking of her role in this way requires her to focus on doing her work in a way that helps others to do theirs.

The power of this outward-mindset approach can be seen in the results of an innovative debt-collection agency that has built its entire mission and strategy in the way depicted in the outward-mindset-at-work diagram. The company is CFS2, headquartered in Tulsa, Oklahoma.

Bill Bartmann, founder and CEO of CFS2, who died unexpectedly in 2016, knew his own hard times. A controversial figure in many respects, Bill had a professional life that was a roller-coaster ride of exhilarating climbs and dramatic falls, including bankruptcy and criminal charges (for which he was exonerated on all counts). With his ups and downs, Bill has both fans and naysayers. Nevertheless, following the bankruptcy of his first debt-collection venture, he set out to build a debt-collection company that worked differently—which is to say, outwardly.

Bill and his company focus on treating those who are in debt with dignity and respect. They operate from the premise that their clients owe them money precisely because *they don't have enough money to pay them*. The typical approach to debt collection—an inward-mindset approach—is to browbeat those who owe money until you squeeze whatever you can out of them. An outward-mindset approach, on the other hand, begins with thinking about these people and what they are up against. Those who take this approach are alive to and interested in the challenges these people are facing, and their mission is to help them with those challenges.

With this approach, Bill Bartmann and his people began collecting debt not by squeezing their clients for money but by figuring out how they could help them *make money*. Bill asked his entire workforce to begin brainstorming and experimenting to see how they could best help their clients get jobs. At first, they tried giving their clients advice and suggestions about what to do. But this didn't seem to help much. They huddled as a company to figure out how to be more helpful, and one of Bill's employees offered this observation: "They can't do the heavy lifting themselves—they're so beat down they have no get-up-and-go left."[1]

So the employees of CFS2 began writing résumés for their clients. They began looking for job opportunities for them, helping them fill out applications, and scheduling job interviews. They ran mock interviews with their clients to prepare them for the real thing. And they even began calling their clients on the mornings of their appointments to get them out of bed early enough to arrive at the job interview on time!

From there they began helping in other ways. Any headache in their clients' lives became an opportunity to help. In an interview with *Harvard Business Review*, Bill talked about how they get requests for all kinds of help—from food stamps to child care to home repairs.[2] CFS2 has identified a myriad of organizations that exist to help people in need with these and many other services, and Bill's team brings in these organizations to help meet the needs of their clients. And they do all this for free. In fact, CFS2 rewards its employees not for how much debt they collect but for how many free services they can provide to their clients!

From an inward-mindset perspective, this all seems crazy. But the results speak for themselves. After just three years in the industry, CFS2's rate of collection was two times that of any firm in the industry.[3] Clients feel helped by the people at CFS2— some even financially rescued by them. And because their clients have money they didn't have before, they have resources to pay to CFS2. CFS2 has become a partner—even a friend—that they *want* to pay. The approach was so revolutionary that Bill was nominated for a Nobel Peace Prize.

We see in the CFS2 story how an outward-mindset approach can mobilize an entire company to work on behalf of its customers—not just to provide a product or service but to enthusiastically innovate to meet the customers' needs and help them achieve their own objectives. Inward-mindset people and organizations *do* things. Outward-mindset people and organizations *help others to be able to do things.*

CFS2 provides a good example of an outward-mindset approach with external customers. The same approach can be applied inside organizations—toward peers, direct reports, and managers.

Consider the example of the longtime NBA juggernaut, the San Antonio Spurs. One day, time will catch up with them, and they will suffer through a challenging rebuilding process, but they have avoided that inevitable downturn longer than any other franchise in the modern era. Although recent challenges have knocked them down a notch, the Spurs have remained dominant in the NBA long past the time many predicted they would decline. They have been able to do this despite the aging of key players, the annual turnover of many members of the team, and would-be challengers that have fallen and risen and fallen again. When you play the Spurs, you play a dynamically adaptive outward-mindset organism. We say *organism* because they are so alive to each other that they appear to act as a single entity. When you watch them play, you notice that the ball doesn't stick in the hands of any player. The moment it would be more advantageous for the ball to be somewhere else, the ball moves there. There is no ego on the floor that keeps the most advantageous moves from happening.

When asked what kinds of qualities the Spurs look for in players, Coach Gregg Popovich says that they look for players who "have gotten over themselves."[4] A FOXBusiness article expands on this comment and explores how the Spurs' outward-mindset culture gives them a significant competitive advantage.[5] The author attributes the Spurs' success to four factors: (1) recruiting for and building selflessness and teamwork—what Coach Popovich calls "relationship excellence," (2) caring for players and staff as people, (3) giving players and staff a voice, and (4) achieving task excellence that is enabled by relationship excellence. "We are disciplined," Coach Popovich says, "but that's not enough. Relationships with people are what it's all about. You have to make players realize you care about them. And they have to care about each other and be interested in each other."[6]

This commitment to each other makes the Spurs players feel a heightened obligation to build their skills and consistently perform at their best. Why? Because that is what their teammates need from them. Their teammates *need* them to become the best they can be. And with an outward mindset, the players feel an obligation to help *each other* get better. They owe that to one another.

"Popovich understands," the author of the article writes, "that without relationship excellence, task excellence and superior results are built on feet of clay. Because he intentionally develops relationship excellence among the team, the Spurs are able to achieve task excellence and sustainable superior performance."[7]

The Spurs' coaches and players demonstrate that people are able to achieve far greater results than they alone would be willing or able to do precisely because they have committed themselves to something that is bigger than themselves—an organizational and interpersonal cause that requires the best of each of them. All the members of the Spurs organization—from the general manager to coaches to players—help *each other* succeed. A lot of teams—most, in fact—are filled with people interested in their own success. Such teams won't be able to approach the Spurs' level of sustained success until all individual contributors become as interested in their colleagues' success as they are their own.

9. THE OUTWARD-MINDSET PATTERN

In chapter 8 we introduced the outward-mindset way of thinking about one's role and obligations at work (and elsewhere). A hallmark of this way of working is a focus on the needs, objectives, and challenges of those toward whom one has responsibility. Over the years, we have discovered that those who work with an outward mindset exhibit a particular pattern—a three-part approach that can be implemented to turn individuals, teams, and organizations outward.

DIAGRAM 12. **THE OUTWARD-MINDSET PATTERN**

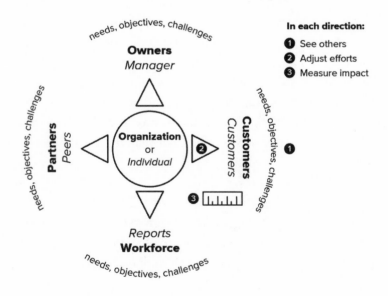

As outlined in diagram 12, people who consistently work with an outward mindset excel in three ways that those who work with an inward mindset do not. They

1. see the needs, objectives, and challenges of others
2. adjust their efforts to be more helpful to others
3. measure and hold themselves accountable for the impact of their work on others

Engaging in these three steps is a practical approach to implementing and sustaining an outward-mindset way of working. You can remember the pattern with the simple acronym SAM—see others, adjust efforts, measure impact. We capture this outward-mindset pattern in diagram 12 on the next page.

The power of the outward-mindset pattern can be seen in the turnaround of Ford Motor Company, a change that began with the hiring of a new CEO—Alan Mulally.

Mulally spent thirty-seven years at Boeing, where he was instrumental in turning around Boeing's commercial-jetliner business. A native Kansan with a disarming "aw-shucks" manner coupled with steely perseverance and an innate knack for team building, he was hired as president and CEO at Ford in September 2006. The company was in a desperate state. Bleeding at the rate of $17 billion per year, it put all its remaining chips on Alan Mulally.[1]

As Mulally soon discovered, no one at Ford felt responsible for the problems of the company. The situation was like what we find with organizations generally—people usually rate themselves much more favorably than they rate their companies. Ford was losing billions of dollars annually while the individuals at the company believed they themselves were performing well (or at least not as poorly as their colleagues).

Mulally brought to Ford the management approach that had been so successful for him at Boeing. He led through a mechanism of two weekly meetings. The first, the Business Plan Review, or BPR, as it is commonly referred to at Ford, is held every Thursday morning. Immediately following the BPR, the leaders reconvene in a second meeting, the Special Attention Review, or SAR, to devise tactical solutions for the issues identified during the BPR.

Mulally trained his executive team to come to the BPR prepared with charts that showed performance against the company plan for each area of responsibility. He had them color-code their charts: Anything that was on plan was to be coded green, anything at risk of going off plan was to be coded yellow, and anything off plan was to be coded red. Changes from the prior week were to be coded blue. They couldn't have anyone else report for them; each member of the executive team was responsible for his or her own part of the business. "This is the only way I know how to operate," Mulally explained to his team in their introductory meeting. "We need to have everybody involved. We need to have a plan. And we need to know where we are on the plan."[2] Mulally pointed to ten BPR rules he had posted on the wall of the room[3]:

- People first
- Everyone is included
- Compelling vision
- Clear performance goals
- One plan
- Facts and data

- Propose a plan, "find-a-way" attitude
- Respect, listen, help, and appreciate each other
- Emotional resilience . . . trust the process
- Have fun . . . enjoy the journey and each other

Most of the executives were not very keen on Mulally's weekly reporting mechanism. One even walked out on the first week's meeting, chafing at what sounded like an overload of unhelpful weekly meeting prep.[4] Dutifully, however, all the team members came the next week with charts prepared. The company was losing money hand over fist, but as the executives presented, each and every chart was coded green.

Why, despite the company's woeful performance, were all the charts green? Because you couldn't be wrong at Ford and keep your position. So no one was wrong. *The company was underperforming, sure,* the executives would privately admit, *but I'm not. Jason might be, or Beth, or Ash, but not me. At least I'm performing at a higher level than they are. The situation would be a lot worse if not for me.*

Mulally was troubled by the sea of green charts, but he wasn't surprised by it. He was new, and the team was still unsure about him. He understood that. But he also knew that this couldn't continue for long if the company was going to survive. He continued his daily work with the team in part so they would know that it was safe for them to present the truth. But when they convened again the next two weeks, the charts were still green. By halfway through the third week's meeting, Mulally had seen enough. "We're going to lose billions of dollars this year," he said, interrupting the reporting. "Is there anything that's *not* going well here?"[5]

His team nervously looked at the boardroom tabletop. No one said anything.

The next week, just before the new Ford Edge was about to ship out of Oakville, Ontario, Canada, a test driver reported a problem on one of the test vehicles: the tailgate had an actuator problem. Mark Fields had a decision to make.

Fields led Ford's operations in the Americas. Had the company promoted from within, he would have been the new CEO instead of Mulally. So Fields figured that his days at Ford were numbered. With these facts in mind, he weighed his options. *The problem on the tailgate may well turn out to be an anomaly,* he thought. *We could ship and everything would be fine.* On the other hand, if the vehicles weren't fine, it would be big trouble. Mulally was demanding that everything Ford produced be first in class. Shiny new Ford Edges with faulty tailgates would create a very public counterpoint. Not knowing the new boss well yet, Fields knew he couldn't take that chance. So he would postpone the launch. He had settled it in his mind.

That left a more difficult decision: Was he going to tell anyone about the problem at the Thursday BPR? Again, he weighed his options. *We can probably get this fixed and ship the cars without anyone knowing about the issue. On the other hand, what if we can't?* That thought suggested that he tell Mulally and his colleagues the truth. But this kind of transparency wasn't safe at Ford at the time. Telling the truth, exposing challenges in your area of operations, usually resulted in losing your job. These were hard-charging professionals for whom other people's mistakes were like chum to sharks. Fields felt like a dead man. If he shipped and the vehicles were faulty, he was a goner. But he was sure that the same fate awaited him if he came to the meeting and, in a final blaze of glory, told everyone that the Edge had a problem.

He thought it over and finally decided that since he was dead anyway, he was going to call it like it was. He prepared his chart. In red.

Fields filed into the room on week four as the only person on the team with a chart that was anything but green. When it was his turn, he tried to be nonchalant. When the Ford Edge chart came up, he said, "And on the Edge, we're red; you can see it there."

Silence.

Everyone around the table knew what Mark Fields knew. He was as good as gone.

Everyone except one, and that person started clapping. "Mark," Mulally smiled as he clapped, "that is great visibility." Then he turned to the rest of the group and asked the question that was the beginning of their education in the outward mindset: "Who can help Mark with that?"

At that invitation, a number of Fields's colleagues jumped in with offers. One said that he had seen that issue on another vehicle and would get that information to Fields immediately. Another offered to quickly get a group of his top flight engineers to Oakville to help on any redesign that might need to happen. And so on.

Interestingly, in the BPR the following week, Fields was still the only person with a chart that was anything but green. No one was yet willing to follow his lead and give an honest accounting because everyone had expected him to be dismissed after the prior week's meeting. When he showed up the following week with his Edge chart still red, but moving to yellow, and Mulally still smiling at him, the others began to realize that Mulally was for real. "*You* aren't red," Mulally insisted. "The issue you're working on is red." And he wanted them to help each other with the challenges they each faced, something they could do only if they came forward with their challenges. The week after that, the charts around the room had so much red that the meeting looked like a crime scene.[6]

The team continued to work this way together, regularly reporting on their responsibilities and learning about the challenges their colleagues were facing. "Who can help with that?" was as common a question as the charts were red and yellow. Individually and collectively, team members stayed focused on nailing their own responsibilities and doing so in ways that helped their colleagues nail theirs. They tracked not only what they each did but also their impact on each other and their various stakeholders.

You may know the rest of the story. Working this way together and spreading this helpful, self-accountable approach throughout the company, Ford was able to pull itself out of a deep ditch—to such a degree that it was able to get in front of the financial crisis of 2007–08 as the only American automobile manufacturer that didn't have to take federal moneys to survive. Alan Mulally retired from Ford in the spring of 2014 and joined the board of Google.

Think about the Ford turnaround story in relation to the three elements of the outward-mindset pattern that we diagrammed earlier in the chapter.

Regarding the first step—*seeing the needs, objectives, and challenges of others* (and the organization as a whole)—the BPR process itself gave the members of Mulally's team visibility both into their own contribution to the whole and into the needs, objectives, challenges, and activities of their colleagues. It was up to each person to engage in the process with an outward mindset, which took a while to happen at Ford. Had Mulally not run the BPR process with an outward mindset himself, the process would not have yielded the benefit we are speaking of here. But because Mulally's mindset was outward in the way he worked with his team and conducted these meetings, that forum offered the Ford team an opportunity to see their own roles in relation to others.

The second step of the outward-mindset pattern is *adjusting one's work to become more helpful to others*. This step naturally follows the first. Once the team could see the challenges faced around the table, Mulally invited them to step up and help. "Who can help Mark with that?" was more than a question. It was a statement about how Mulally wanted his people to take responsibility not just for their own part in the overall project but also for their impact on their colleagues' ability to successfully fulfill their responsibilities.

Lastly, they gathered together each week to see if the help they were providing was making any difference in their coworkers' ability to get results. This is the third step in the outward-mindset pattern: *measuring impact*. Mulally's process gave the Ford team at least a once-a-week way of assessing whether the adjustments being made by those around the room were actually helping. Each week they had the opportunity to assess their impact on one another and the company's overall results and make necessary adjustments.

You see the same outward-mindset pattern at play in the example of the debt collection agency, CFS2, that we discussed in chapter 8. The company was founded upon the outward-mind-set pattern. The initial team began by trying to *see others*—to see and understand their debtors or customers. They quickly real-ized that the main reason these people owed them money was because they didn't have any. Their greatest need was money.

With this understanding, the team moved to the *adjust efforts* step in the pattern by asking this question: What could we do to help these people make money? Consider the significance of this. Before this moment, do you suppose any debt-collection agency in the history of the world had ever organized its efforts in response to such a question?

But the CFS2 team didn't stop at instituting what they thought were good, helpful ideas. They measured what worked and what didn't. Which is to say, they instituted the third step in the out-ward-mindset pattern: *measure impact*. Measuring the impact of their efforts to help their clients make money helped them see and understand them even more, which naturally led to more adjustments, which they then tracked and measured, and so on.

The turnaround at Ford and the success of CFS2 depended on the teams engaging in each step of the outward-mindset pat-tern: see others, adjust efforts, and measure impact. In the next chapter, we take a deeper look at each of these three elements of the pattern.

10. APPLYING THE OUTWARD-MINDSET PATTERN

In chapter 9 we introduced the outward-mindset pattern—see others, adjust efforts, and measure impact. In this chapter we will explore how to begin using this approach by sharing how different individuals and organizations have successfully implemented the three elements of this pattern.

See Others

A few years ago, Arbinger was engaged by a large power company to help find ways to save time and money by reducing the inordinate amount of time leaders spent each year mired in planning the next year's capital budget.

We spent about thirty minutes breaking down the budgeting process into its component parts. The forty or so leaders in the room gathered into groups or teams that were responsible for each part in the process: the planners formed one team, engineers another, and so on. On the whiteboard-paint walls, each team constructed an outward-mindset diagram for that group's step in the budgeting process. The teams wrote their part of the process in the center. In a circle around that, they listed the names of the people and groups that they affected in the budgeting process. They then drew triangles facing outward in each direction and wrote next to each group what they understood of their needs, objectives, and challenges.

After a few minutes, the walls were covered with diagrams that looked something like diagram 13.

All members of the various groups circulated around the room to see if they should add their own or others' names to any of the diagrams or whether they should add any key needs, objectives, or challenges that weren't yet listed. Everyone had free rein to amend any diagram.

Seeing themselves correctly in relation to others, the leaders were now positioned to begin seeing others more clearly than before. They only needed to start looking. We invited the teams to take turns at the front of the room. Everyone else was given

DIAGRAM 13. **THE OUTWARD-MINDSET PROJECT**

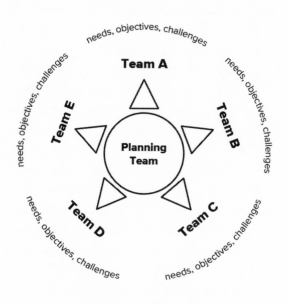

the opportunity to ask questions of each group to learn as much as possible about that team's needs, objectives, challenges, and activities.

The first group was the Planning team. Planning initiates the budgeting process at the beginning of every year by looking at projected community energy-consumption needs and energy-production possibilities and ultimately arriving at a mix of projects that would need to be engineered and constructed in the following year. This process took four months. Historically, the planners had passed their plans to the next group, the Engineering team, on May 1. In turn, the engineers would take two and a half months to design the projects and then pass their work to the people who handled step three of the process, and so on.

Something interesting happened when people began asking questions to more fully see and understand the needs and objectives of the planners: the planners immediately became interested in the needs and objectives of their questioners as well. What started as a question-and-answer session evolved into a conversation in the middle of which the group made a startling discovery: the planners knew 80 to 90 percent of the projects that would go in the final plan by mid-January. It took another three and a half months to finalize the last 10 to 20 percent. When the planners saw this, they suddenly knew an obvious way to shave three months off the budgeting timeline: the planners would no longer hold the whole batch of projects until all of them were finalized. Beginning immediately, they would forward the individual projects that would go into the final plan as soon as they knew them. This meant that Engineering could start its part of the process in January rather than May. This change made a huge difference. And that was just the first group.

Why couldn't that change have happened earlier? It could have, of course. These were highly competent people. But without a framework that makes the solutions that already exist in an organization discoverable, many tremendously helpful solutions lie dormant. It's as if an organization consists of many potential Bluetooth connections, most of which have not been turned on. When you make those devices discoverable to each other, they can begin to talk. And when they do, they figure out how to make things better. You can make them discoverable by instituting opportunities to *see others*. This was one of the main benefits of the BPR process that Alan Mulally instituted at Ford, as we discussed in chapter 9. The weekly meetings provided an occasion for the Ford executive team to learn to see each other.

Our research shows that one of the most accurate indicators of mindset in organizations is lateral awareness—that is, the extent to which people are aware of the needs, objectives, and challenges of individuals and teams lateral to them in the company. When people have an inward mindset, self-interest might compel them to learn about the objectives of their bosses or the activities of those who report to them. But self-interest alone does not normally invite people to learn more about those situated laterally to them. That is why lateral awareness is such a good indicator of mindset. Accordingly, efforts to see others and increase horizontal awareness within and across teams is a key strategy both for helping people become aware of the inwardness that has characterized an organization and for helping individuals, teams, and entire organizations break free from the inward-mindset box.

Journalist Brenda Ueland, in her insightful essay on listening, "Tell Me More: On the Fine Art of Listening," provides interesting insight regarding the simple potency of trying to "see others" through listening. "Listening is a magnetic and strange thing, a creative force," she writes. "Think how the friends that really listen to us are the ones we move toward, and we want to sit in their radius as though it did us good, like ultraviolet rays. This is the reason: When we are listened to, it creates us, makes us unfold and expand. Ideas actually begin to grow within us and come to life."[1]

Ueland then describes the difference between how she used to interact with others and how she learned to interact with people after she learned to be interested in them. Think about how her description of her former way summarizes so much of what happens in the sales processes of organizations and in company meetings, as well as in interactions in our social lives: "Before . . . when I went to a party I would think anxiously, 'Now try hard. Be lively. Say bright things. Talk. Don't let down.' And when tired, I would have to drink a lot of coffee to keep this up. Now before going to a party I just tell myself to listen with affection to anyone who talks to me, to be in their shoes when they talk; to try to know them without my mind pressing against theirs, or arguing, or changing the subject. No. My attitude is, 'Tell me more.'"[2]

Rob Dillon experienced the same kind of shift that Brenda Ueland did. Rob is the fourth-generation member of his family to lead Dillon Floral, a wholesale florist that serves Pennsylvania and neighboring Eastern Seaboard states. His company faces a challenging market, as its historical customers, small local florists, have been declining steadily in number with the rise of the superstores that sell flowers. To retain its shrinking customer base, Dillon Floral included in-person customer visits as an important part of its strategy. But Rob detested these visits. He knew that his customers were struggling, and he didn't like how he felt walking into the stores of struggling customers and trying to persuade them to buy this or that Dillon Floral product. Consequently, over the years, Rob made fewer and fewer visits — until, that is, he learned the power of really seeing others that Ueland writes about.

Rob disliked engaging with his customers because he had been making self-focused visits rather than others-focused visits. He had mainly been interested in trying to get the people he was calling on to buy his products. He interacted with his customers in the same way Ueland interacted in social gatherings before she learned simply to get interested in and be open to others. Rob felt the pressure to perform, to impress, to sell. "I used to walk into meetings with customers with an agenda," he said, "and I had a whole bunch of fear." He says that when he learned just to get interested in seeing others, this all changed.

Today when Rob calls on customers, his only thought is, *How can I help?* He isn't there to impress the customers, and he certainly doesn't perform. He just wants to figure out what he can do to help them, and that starts with seeing — trying to understand the needs, objectives, and challenges of others. With this new focus, Rob now spends one to two days every week calling on customers. He's been surprised to discover that he loves it. As a direct result of this, clients that had quit purchasing from Dillon Floral have since returned, and many that had been thinking of turning elsewhere instead felt a renewed commitment to their partnership.

Rob describes the change this way: "Since learning about the outward mindset, I simply go into meetings with customers wanting to learn whatever I can about their needs, objectives, and challenges. I would rather walk into a flower shop stupid than smart. I say to them that I want to learn how we could be more helpful to them. And then I just listen. Seeing them as people, I can very easily empathize with them no matter what they say. There is nothing to fear. I'm just there to help."

This comment is revealing. When, with an outward mindset, Rob is really interested in seeing others, he naturally feels a desire to find ways to be more helpful—which brings us to the second step in the outward-mindset pattern: adjusting our efforts.

Adjust Efforts

A longtime colleague of ours, Terry Olson, tells of the following experience that began in a workshop he was conducting for public-school teachers. They were using a room at a lockdown educational facility for elementary-aged children with severe behavioral problems. Some of the teachers from that school were eavesdropping at the back of the room.

In the middle of the presentation, one of these teachers at the back asked a question about how to handle a boy who was becoming increasingly unmanageable. In fact, although they had frequently used the "time-out" room (a small, locked, carpeted cubicle used to isolate disruptive children) to discipline the boy, he seemed to be getting worse. He would settle down briefly after a time-out experience and then would become even more disruptive than before. The most dramatic of his antics had occurred the prior week, when a serviceman delivering soda to the vending machines left a school door open while he maneuvered a loaded hand truck inside. The unmanageable boy, Toby, had just bolted from his classroom (a frequent occurrence) and was hiding in the refreshment area when the delivery gave him the opportunity to escape. Running out into the schoolyard, Toby tore off all his clothes and began running through the park. Before long, Toby, naked, was being chased down by a score of panicked teachers.

"So, what do you do with a student like that?" the teacher asked.

Terry told the questioner that he had no magic solution but suggested that if the boy became increasingly unmanageable after being locked in the time-out room, maybe he was not responding to the particular punishment as much as he was rebelling against being seen and treated like an object. "Objects do what you want them to do," Terry explained. "You can throw a washcloth in the sink, kick a soccer ball across a field, or push clothes into a laundry bag. But when you try to throw, kick, or push people, they often resist. Toby might be resisting the idea of being a 'thing.'"

Terry suggested to the teachers that if none of their disciplinary techniques were working with Toby, perhaps they should consider a different approach. Instead of chasing him down when he bolted from class and putting him in the time-out room, Terry invited them to imagine new possibilities. He said, "What if you asked this question of yourselves: If I were to give my heart to this boy, what would occur to me to do?" He then invited them to act on what occurred to them to do.

Two weeks later, Terry was back in the facility for another workshop session. He wondered what, if anything, had developed with Toby. The teachers from the school were eager to report. One woman recounted the following experience:

Toby ran out of my room two days after we had talked, and instead of sending my aide after him immediately, I continued teaching. After a few minutes, I turned the class over to my aide and went looking for Toby myself. I found him in the auditorium, "hiding" under a blanket. Toby hid as many second graders do—his leg was sticking out from under the blanket. I asked myself that question, "If I were to give my heart to this boy, what would occur to me to do?" Immediately, I thought of those days as a child when I had played hide-and-go-seek. Almost on an impulse, I sat down on the floor. I said, "Hi, Toby. I can't play hide-and-go seek with you now; I've got a class to teach. But if you still want to play when it's recess, I will come and find you."

At recess I went back to the auditorium. It seemed he had not moved. I pulled the blanket off and said, "Found you!" I then explained I wanted to be "it" and threw the blanket over *my* head. "I'll count to twenty-five," I said. He stood there until I got to ten. Then he hesitatingly ran out of the auditorium. I searched. I found him in a classroom pressed into a vertical broom closet. I started counting again. I found him for the third time as the bell rang. I explained that I had to go teach now.

Twenty minutes later he almost sneaked into my classroom and slid into his chair. He has not been perfect, but I have been different. When he misbehaves, that question of yours has become an echo in my brain: "If I were to give my heart . . . ?" Sometimes I stop everything and ask him a question. Sometimes I ask him to help someone else. Sometimes I explain that I need help. Sometimes I explain to him that he just "can't do that," and I go on. He settles down. It is a day-by-day thing, but I am different with him. He seems different to me, even when he acts up.

This teacher discovered what all outward individuals and organizations know: real helpfulness can't be made into a formula. To be outward doesn't mean that people should adopt this or that prescribed behavior. Rather, it means that when people see the needs, challenges, desires, and humanity of others, the most effective ways to adjust their efforts occur to them in the moment. When they see others as people, they respond in human and helpful ways. They naturally adjust what they do in response to the needs they see around them. With an outward mindset, adjusting one's efforts naturally follows from seeing others in a new way.

This brings us to the third element of the outward-mindset pattern — measuring one's impact on others.

Measure Impact

For people who are implementing the outward-mindset pattern, what might *measuring impact* look like? And how might a person or organization go about doing it? Consider the following stories.

Attorney Charles Jackson, a third-year associate lawyer at a midsized law firm, was attending a leadership course we were conducting. Charles spent about 90 percent of his time working on issues for clients that had been brought to the firm by partners in the firm. He spent the other 10 percent of his time on client work he himself had generated for the firm. As we discussed working with an outward mindset, Charles could not get two of his own clients out of his mind. Both of them were unhappy with the job Charles had done. But until that moment, Charles hadn't been overly concerned about this. *Not every client is going to be happy with you,* he had assured himself. *There's nothing you can do about that. Besides, I did the work, even if they weren't happy with some aspects of it.* During the workshop, we presented the idea that working with an outward mindset requires that people take responsibility not just for what they do but also for the impact of what they do. As Charles began considering this idea, these client situations started to seem a bit different to him.

One of the clients had been unhappy with how long it had taken Charles to handle his issue. Until then, Charles had brushed the complaint away. As he now thought about it, however, he realized that his client had a legitimate gripe. Charles hadn't given the work high enough priority, and his slow pace had created difficulties for his client that he had never apologized for or addressed.

The second client had been surprised by the bill Charles sent him. Charles hated talking about billing and had avoided the conversation altogether with this client. The first time the client learned about Charles's cost was when he received the invoice Charles had sent.

As Charles considered his impact on these clients, he felt he should return their money. So he did. One of these clients lived in a different state, so Charles wrote a letter of apology and enclosed it with a check. The other client lived in Charles's city, so Charles offered his apology and delivered the check in person.

How many times do you suppose attorneys have willingly and on their own returned the money clients have paid them?

Charles returned the money in May of that year, and he began tracking his impact on his clients by checking in with them on a regular basis to make sure that he was meeting or exceeding their expectations. Then something interesting happened. These clients started talking to their friends and acquaintances about their honest and conscientious lawyer. By July, Charles was receiving seven new client matters per week. By November, that number had grown to thirteen per week, and Charles was employing three of his law-firm colleagues nearly full-time on client work he had brought in. In March, he left his job to start his own law firm.

All of this happened because Charles made a disciplined effort to track and hold himself accountable for his impact on his clients. He called his regular check-ins with his clients *self-accountability checks*. This approach to measuring one's impact requires nothing but a willingness to stay in regular conversations with others about whether they feel one's efforts are helping them or not.

Another way to measure impact is to find metrics that show a person or organization what others are able to accomplish or achieve as a result of their efforts. This was what a nonprofit organization called Hope Arising found a way to do.

Hope Arising is dedicated to assisting orphaned and at-risk children in rural Ethiopia. Eager to meet an urgent need for clean water in the drought-stricken areas where these children live, the team diligently worked to improve their ability to deliver more and more clean water. Naturally, they measured efforts in terms of their output: gallons of clean water delivered.

When the Hope Arising team learned about the outward-mindset pattern, they saw that although they had discovered a need and were working on adjusting their efforts to meet that need, they had never thought about how to measure the *impact* of their work. Consequently, they didn't actually know whether they were meeting the needs of the orphaned and at-risk children they were trying to help. They began to consider how they could measure their actual impact.

They knew that they needed to assess what was happening on the ground. "What kind of metric," one team member asked, "would show us our *impact* and not just our *output?*" "What impact do the people *want?*" another responded. "What are they hoping clean water will do for them? If we had answers to those kinds of questions, maybe we could figure out what we should be measuring."

With these questions in mind, the team started talking to villagers across the region. In hut after hut they heard the same thing: "We need clean water because we need our kids to be able to go to school. When our kids are sick from dirty water, they miss school. And if kids can't go to school, the traveling schoolteachers don't get paid. So they move on to other villages. But if our kids don't get educated, they'll never escape this poverty."

This was a revelation to the Hope Arising team in two ways. First of all, they had found a way to measure their impact: number of days children are in school. Measuring this would show them their impact on what mattered most to the recipients of their services, and they could easily get this data from local governments. The second revelation was this: they weren't really in the water-delivery business; they were in the helping-kids-get-to-school business. This realization got them thinking about all kinds of ways they could be helping in addition to ensuring the delivery of clean water.

As Hope Arising discovered, engaging in the first two steps of the outward-mindset pattern is not enough. If we don't measure the impact of our efforts on the objectives of those we are serving, we will remain blind to important ways we need to adjust and will end up not serving others well.

11. DON'T WAIT ON OTHERS

If you have read either *Leadership and Self-Deception* or *The Anatomy of Peace*, you will be familiar with the character named Lou Herbert. The inspiration for the Lou character was a man named Jack Hauck, the founder and longtime CEO of Tubular Steel, a St. Louis–based national distributor of steel and carbon products. Tubular had engaged one of the world's best-known consultants to help it overcome the toxic infighting that plagued the senior management team and stymied the growth of the entire company. After months of trying one approach after another without success, Jack asked this consultant if he knew of any other approach the company could try. The consultant was acquainted with Arbinger's work and recommended that Jack explore our ideas.

During our first meeting with Jack and his team, we focused on helping each executive team member reassess his or her contribution to the challenges the company faced by carefully considering the following statement: *As far as I am concerned, the problem is me.*

As eager as Jack was to solve his company's problems, he struggled early on to apply this statement to himself. "I want you all to get the message," he said. "I'm going to have posters made and put up all over the building." Then, pointing his finger at the assembled executives and officers, he said, "Don't forget: *As far as you are concerned, the problem is you.*" Eyes rolled, and people dropped their shaking heads into their hands. It is so easy to leave oneself out of the equation when considering an organization's problems, even without realizing one is doing so.

Even though the issues at Tubular were not simply the problems of a single person, it was clear that no problem could be solved if individuals were not willing to address how they themselves were part of the problem. If you recall the Ford story from chapter 9, you'll remember that the unwillingness of team members to step forward and admit their contribution to the company's problems was the primary issue that Alan Mulally had to crack before anything could improve. Given the history at Ford, turning outward seemed too personally risky at the time for most members of the leadership team—so risky, in fact, that they had, in essence, decided that they would rather the company fail than admit and address their contributions to its problems. That is, until one person was willing to make the first move and turn outward without any assurance of what others would do.

So while the goal in shifting mindsets is to get everyone turned toward each other, accomplishing this goal is possible only if people are prepared to turn their mindsets toward others with no expectation that others will change their mindsets in return.

This capability—to change the way I see and work with others regardless of whether they change—overcomes the biggest impediment to mindset change: the natural, inward-mindset inclination to wait for others to change before doing anything different oneself. This is the natural trap in organizations. Executives want employees to change, and employees wait on their leaders. Parents want change in their children, and children wait for the same in their parents. Spouses wait on change in each other.

Everyone waits.

So nothing happens.

Ironically, the most important move in mindset work is to make the move one is waiting for the *other* to make. Diagram 14 illustrates this move.

The top of the diagram depicts two people—me and another—whose mindsets are mutually inward. Both of us have, in effect, turned our backs to the other's needs and objectives. From this stance, each of us is waiting to be seen by the other. I want the other person to begin to see and consider *me*—*my* views, objectives, and needs. On some level I may

DIAGRAM 14. **THE MOST IMPORTANT MOVE**

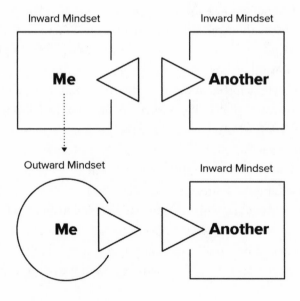

realize that the other person wants the same from me, but for the reasons discussed in chapter 6, I resist.

The *most important move* consists of my putting down my resistance and beginning to act in the way I want the other person to act. This move is depicted in the bottom half of the diagram, which illustrates what should be the main goal of any effort to change mindset: to equip people to change their own mindsets even when others are not yet ready or willing to change theirs.

Would our organizations be better off if all of us were to turn outward in our work with each other? Yes. But this preferred state can be reached only if some are willing to change even when others do not—and to sustain the change whether or not others reciprocate.

This kind of unilateral change is the essence of true leadership. Unfortunately, those who make this move are too rare. People tend not to make this move precisely because the inwardness of those with whom they are engaged gives them all the justification they need to stay inward themselves. At Tubular, Jack Hauck's inward mindset toward his leadership team provided them with every justification to further entrench themselves in the self-focused, protective, and frequently combative posture they had adopted. And no one was more so entrenched than Jack's right-hand man and chief of staff, Larry Heitz.

Unbeknownst to Jack, at the time of our first meeting with the team, Larry had already made plans to leave the company. After years of dealing with Jack, he had decided that enough was enough and that Jack would never change. The only sensible choice was to move on. Since Larry had learned that the head of sales felt the same way, they had begun quietly recruiting the company's best and brightest to defect and start a competitor organization.

Shaken by Larry's departure, Jack began to consider how he might be complicit in the problems that plagued his company. The scrutiny he had once applied to his people, he refocused on himself. He started to change, both at home and at work.

As Larry built his new company, he heard about the efforts Jack was making to change the way he engaged with others as a leader. This caused Larry to consider all that he had learned from Jack while at Tubular—lessons that had proved vital in the success of Larry's new company. With a promising prospective buyer for his company, Larry began to wonder what it might be like to rejoin Jack.

One year after Larry had left, he picked up the phone to call him. "Jack, it's Larry," he said. "I've been thinking a lot since I left. You've invested a lot in me over the years, and everything I know, I learned from you. I've used what you've taught me to build my own company, and I think I could help you turn Tubular around. I don't know if you'd be willing to let me return, but I'd really like to come back and work together to try to save the company."

Remarkably, Jack agreed.

Larry returned, dedicating his full-time efforts working with a small Arbinger team to develop and implement a systematic outward approach across the entire organization. As a result of this work, one person and department at a time began to turn outward. This took discipline.

One enduring fight in the company was the daily battle between the sales and credit departments. Both had a compelling story to share. (And share they did!)

The credit department, charged to keep bad debt below 2.5 percent of the company's revenue, felt responsible to scrutinize each credit application and deny most of them. The credit team had learned to watch the salespeople carefully, knowing that in their push to get a sale they would try to slide credit risks by them, go around them to get exceptions from the executive team, or turn the application in right before the sales deadline so that there wouldn't be enough time to research the applicant.

Of course, the problem seemed very different from the perspective of the sales team. Just as they were ready to close a big sale, the credit people would deny the customer's application on a technicality—rules or policies that seemed ever changing and never communicated. With compensation largely tied to commissions, the sales team felt undermined at every turn.

"Don't they get that we don't have revenue if we don't have sales?" the exasperated sales team would say.

"But revenue isn't revenue if you can't collect it," the credit team would respond.

Like a never-ending tug-of-war, they were both pulling on separate ends of the same rope, able to achieve their department's objectives only if the other failed to achieve theirs. Each side had justification to spare. Turning outward, it seemed, would mean losing the fight.

But for the first time in his career, Al Klein, the long-standing head of the credit department, wondered whether a fight was actually needed. "We need to be different," he told his team at the beginning of an all-day, closed-door meeting. "I've set aside the entire day today to work on this, and we're not going to leave until we figure out how we can still meet the company's objectives regarding bad debt while enabling the sales team to be successful."

Seeing the needs, challenges, and objectives of the sales team, Al and the credit team began to think more carefully about their role. "The sales team is selling forty different kinds of products," one of them said. "Some are high-margin specialty products, and others are low-margin, high-volume commodities. Surely it would help not only the sales team but the company as a whole if we found ways to approve credit risks for those customers who are making high-margin specialty purchases." Once they started thinking in this way, they devised a completely new objective: maintain bad debt at 2.5 percent of the company's revenues *in a way that helps the sales team achieve their objectives and the company realize its profitability goals.* They also decided that they would check with company leadership to see if a rigid 2.5 percent approach was really best for the company. They wanted to stay open to a better approach.

This newly conceived objective, which now required the credit department to find ways to be helpful to the sales department, called forth a new level of initiative and creativity from the credit team. In less than a week after the credit department made this change, the sales team was overheard to say, "If anyone can figure out how to work with customers to help them qualify, it's our credit team."

Notice the similarity in the ways Jack, Larry, and Al began turning outward despite the inward provocations from others. Considering their impact on others created in each a desire to find ways to be different to improve the results of the company. When they focused on this result, it was no longer Larry versus Jack or credit versus sales. Instead, each began to think about how he might be making it more difficult for the other party to achieve the objectives that the organization required of them. Each did this on his own without requiring the same from the other party. Free of an inward mindset, each was able to see ways to overcome the challenges he had previously faced without demanding that the other reciprocate. For Jack, Larry, and Al, this was the most important move.

As Jack and Larry began focusing on the needs of the company and Al and his credit department team focused on the needs of the sales team, other people across the company began devising and implementing ways of working that were different and far more effective than anything they had ever experienced before. Within two years, Tubular was producing the best return on investment in the industry. Larry, who later succeeded Jack as president, recalled the process this way: "People figured out what they were supposed to do, not only to make their area successful but also to help people in other areas be more successful. Over the course of a few years, that made a tremendous difference to the company and produced a different kind of a culture. As a result, we grew from $30 million to over $100 million and more than quadrupled our profit during a time when the market for our products had gone from about 10 million tons down to 6 million tons. Even in a declining market, we still grew by a factor of four."

None of these results would have happened at Tubular had Jack, Larry, and people like Al waited on others to change. Ironically, only when they gave up their demand that the other parties change were they finally able to see and act in ways that *invited* them to change.

A company that is committed to building an outward-mindset culture will prepare and help people to be able to make and maintain a shift to an outward mindset even when others haven't yet made the shift. Those who persist with an inward mindset ultimately won't be able to stay with such an organization because their staying would not be helpful to them, the organization, or their customers.

The change to an outward mindset doesn't happen overnight. And even where such change is widespread, people who usually operate with an outward mindset will sometimes slip back to an inward mindset. Customers, too, may sometimes have an inward mindset. For all these reasons—as well as because widespread mindset change happens in large measure in response to those who change first—being able to operate with an outward mindset when others do not is a critically important ability. It is *the most important move.*

Sometimes people are afraid to make this move because they think that others may take advantage of them if they do. But people misunderstand the most important move we are talking about if they think that working with an outward mindset when others refuse to do the same makes a person blind to reality or soft on bad behavior. It does neither. In fact, what obscures vision and exposes people to more risk is not an outward mindset, which stays fully alive to and aware of others, but an inward one, which turns its attention away from others while simultaneously provoking resistance. People who work in dangerous, high-risk situations know this most of all—people like the Navy SEALs and SWAT team members we've referenced before. They know that their lives and missions depend on their ability to remain fully aware of the complexities of their situations and to do so in a way that doesn't stir up escalated resistance. The outward mindset doesn't make them soft; it makes them smart.

A related reason why people resist making the most important move is that they think an outward mindset will make them soft when hard behavior is required. But this is a misunderstanding. As we've said, an outward mindset doesn't make people soft; it just makes them open, curious, and aware. Similarly, an inward mindset doesn't make people hard. In fact, people whose mindsets are inward often engage in behaviors that are *softer* than would actually be helpful. Wanting others to think well of them (a common inward-mindset motivation), people often indulge, pacify, or placate others when direct actions would be more helpful. In contrast, parents and leaders who have a responsibility to help others improve and grow may engage in harder behaviors when their mindsets are outward. Why? Because sometimes the help a person needs is a long way from soft. Fear that an outward mindset would make one unhelpfully soft springs from a misconception of this mindset.

Fairly frequently, we encounter leaders who are paralyzed with a different kind of fear. They think that a mindset-change effort might be a good idea, but they worry about how their people will react. So these leaders dip a toe into mindset-change efforts and sit back to see how their people respond. They tell themselves that they will make the decision about whether to proceed with the effort based on the reaction of their people.

In our experience, if people see their leader just dipping a toe in, they will think, rightly, that the effort probably won't amount to much. Consequently, the leader sees a lukewarm response in his or her people and on that basis decides that it probably isn't worth the effort. But that same leader is blind to the biggest reason for the observed reaction: the people have a tepid response because they see the *leader's* tepid response.

Remember, the principle to apply is, *as far as I am concerned, the problem is me. I* am the place to start. Others' responses will depend mostly on what they see in *me.*

The most important move is for *me* to make *the most important move.*

PART III
TURNING TEAMS AND ORGANIZATIONS OUTWARD

12. START WITH MINDSET

Officer Matt Tomasic of the Central Patrol Division of the Kansas City Police Department was finishing his shift on the Kansas City West Side when he witnessed a man assaulting a woman. "Police Department," he shouted. "Take your hands off her and back away." Matt held up his badge. "Do it now!" The man took his hands off the woman, but he didn't back away. "Back away. Now!" Matt shouted. The man turned and started heading toward Matt.

Just then, two cars coming up the road screeched to a halt. The doors flew open and a number of local men bolted from the vehicles. They made a beeline for the man and surrounded him. Their motivation? They wanted to protect Officer Tomasic.

The story of why these men and others in the community were helping the police is a lesson in the helpfulness of starting any change effort with mindset change.

For over fifty years, the corner of Southwest Boulevard and Summit Street in Kansas City and the nearby parking lot of a local liquor store had served as the ad hoc hiring site for day laborers on the city's West Side. This site was in the downtown Hispanic area, which had numerous businesses that catered to the local Hispanic population. For years the numbers of men looking for work were manageable. Those looking for laborers and those looking for labor more or less found what they wanted there. But the numbers of men congregating in this area skyrocketed over a five-year period, and the numbers far exceeded the demand for work.

This swelling group generally consisted of two kinds of men: (1) documented and undocumented men willing to work and (2) documented and undocumented men not interested in working. Those in this second group included a criminal element that gathered to prey on the others. Those who didn't want or couldn't find work loitered around the area. Without available facilities, they urinated on sidewalks and defecated in alleyways. Some would strip naked and shower using the hoses of homeowners. Crime spiked in the area, and businesses started to leave. The community was up in arms.

In response, KCPD tried to manage the situation the way most people do—with behavioral interventions. In this case, it employed overwhelming force and a zero-tolerance policy. Chip Huth's SWAT team was part of this effort before the transformation of Chip and his men that we described in chapter 1. Chip's team members and the other officers deployed in this effort conducted aggressive neighborhood sweeps and arrested large numbers of men for any and every infraction, from drinking in public to all the other laws on the books. But the men arrested typically were back on the same street corner before the day was out. It didn't matter how many resources the department put on the problem. Despite the fifty officers deployed to the West Side, the situation kept getting worse.

Matt had been leading this zero-tolerance approach out of a small community center not too far from the corner of Southwest Boulevard and Summit Street. One day, he was called in to see his KCPD boss, who gave him an ultimatum: "West Side smells like piss, Tomasic. Clean it up. You've got two weeks."

Matt was ready to give up. As he returned to the community center, he thought about how to get moved to an easier assignment, *like Homicide*. He walked into the center to prepare his civilian colleague, Lynda Callon, for his imminent transfer. "I've worked my butt off," he told her, "and things just keep getting worse."

Lynda listened and then said, "Matt, stop being a police officer for a minute and just think about these men. What are their lives like? What do you think it would be like to wonder when you'll work next or to be without basic necessities—without a restroom and not knowing where you'll get your next meal? What would that be like?"

Notice what kinds of questions these were: questions about the needs and objectives of the men they had been trying to change. Lynda had invited Matt to begin thinking and seeing with an outward mindset. In response, Matt, for the first time really, began to consider the issues these men faced.

The community center where Matt and Lynda worked had a restroom and a small stove. Matt and Lynda thought of something simple they could do to help the men with some of their basic needs. They put the word out that the men were welcome to come use the restroom in the center. They also pooled their personal resources to keep a pot of beans on the stove and prepare coffee. This was the beginning of a myriad of changes that Matt and Lynda made to what they had been doing. Once they saw those they had been trying to corral as people, they began to discover ways they could adjust what they were doing to be helpful.

Matt and Lynda soon staged the hiring of day laborers out of the center. Those who didn't find work for the day were invited out into the community to provide neighborhood services—from clearing brush to painting houses to helping neighborhood matriarchs make tamales. Matt spent his time with his sleeves rolled up, engaging in the work right beside these men. They got to know each other, and the men and the community started to trust Matt, which began changing their views of the police. This working side by side provided a way for Matt to see if his approach with the men was really helping them. He started to measure his impact based on the productivity of the men, not how many he took to jail. Based on what he learned, he made further adjustments to be more helpful in his approach.

As this initiative gathered momentum, another officer—Octavio "Chato" Villalobos—heard about the officer who had put a pot of beans on the stove for the people on the West Side, inviting them into the community center to use the restroom. Having grown up on the West Side and knowing about the area's challenges firsthand, Chato was intrigued by what Matt was doing. He asked to be assigned to work with Matt in the neighborhood where he had been raised. On his first day, Chato showed up in full uniform, wearing sunglasses, with extra ammunition and handcuffs hanging off his belt. Matt strongly suggested that, to do the kind of policing that was working on the West Side, Chato go home and change into jeans and a tee shirt.

Since that time, Matt Tomasic and Chato Villalobos have worked together out of the West Side Community Action Network Center in Kansas City. The revitalization of the community has become a national success story. Crime in the area has dropped to an all-time low, and businesses are moving back to the area. These two officers have accomplished what a force of fifty police officers could not—all because they addressed the problem with an outward mindset and did so in a way that invited a change in mindset throughout the community.

"These guys had been around for fifty years on that corner," Chato observes now, still astonished by the changes that have occurred on the West Side. "Matt addressed the issues just by treating people as people—you know, unconditional respect and getting to know who they were and who the bad guys were. It was overwhelming."

The police department's initial response to the challenge on the West Side was to try to clean the problem up with an overwhelming behavioral intervention. The department wanted quick results and deployed overwhelming force to get them. But it didn't work. The West Side changed only because of Matt and Chato's slow work on mindset.

We call mindset work *slow* in this context because too often people who think only of direct behavioral solutions to problems don't understand the need for attention to mindset. They therefore think efforts to shift mindset are a waste of time and would only slow things down. As the approach on Kansas City's West Side demonstrates, they couldn't be more mistaken.

A similar *start-with-mindset* approach was the key to resolving a long-standing labor-management dispute in a large multinational company. We began our work with this organization by spending two days with twenty leaders from the management side of the operation and ten of the labor leaders. During these two days, we helped the team members improve their mindset toward their work and each other. The last hour of the second day was set aside to apply what we had learned together to any particular challenge they were facing.

They told us of a deadlocked labor-management dispute. (We should have been thorough enough in our information gathering to know about this conflict in advance.) The dispute was about to go to arbitration. Despite the high-dollar stakes, labor and management had been unable to find an agreeable way to a resolution over the prior months. The group members said that they wanted to see what they could do to find a way through their impasse in the time we had remaining.

For the first time during our two days together, we split the group into labor and management. We supplied each side with a flip chart and three questions that would help each group to (1) consider the needs, objectives, and challenges of those in the other group, (2) think about what they could adjust to be more helpful to the other group, and (3) consider how they might measure their impact. Twenty minutes later we came back together. We asked one group to present their responses to the first question. Then we invited the other group to present their responses to the same question. We then moved to the second question, reversing the order of the group presentations.

Before we could get to the third question, the presentations evolved into an earnest and very outward discussion, each side showing real interest in and concern for the other's needs and issues. Before forty-five minutes of the hour had passed, the leaders had resolved their conflict. They had done this themselves, with no guidance from us other than the work we had done to prepare them to engage together with an outward mindset and the simple structure we devised for the final exercise. They had resolved their differences in a way that strengthened their working relationship and their trust in each other.

Now it's true that we spent the better part of two days with them to help them get to the point where they could do this. That was the time it took in this case to sufficiently shift mindsets. But if you start with changing mindsets, behavioral transformations can happen quickly. Two days spent working on changing mindsets enabled the leaders to accomplish in forty-five minutes what they had been unable to solve in six months.

Whether in rethinking community policing or resolving labor-management disputes, when people see situations that need to change, the temptation is to immediately apply a behavioral solution. That seems like the fast approach. But if mindset is not addressed, it is usually the *slow* approach to change.

We invite you to do a mindset check before you begin rolling out behavioral solutions. Ask yourself the following questions: Have I (or we) thought this through with an outward mindset? Do I understand the needs, objectives, and challenges of those involved? Have I adjusted my efforts in light of those issues? And have I been holding myself accountable for my impact on these people? Have you considered what mindset-level changes might be necessary in addition to behavioral changes?

You will make progress toward change much more quickly to the degree you first attend to mindset.

13. MOBILIZE AROUND A COLLECTIVE GOAL

Think about the organizations we have discussed in this book that have successfully built outward-mindset cultures. Think about Chip Huth and his SWAT team; Mark Ballif and Paul Hubbard and the fifty healthcare organizations that they have turned around; Louise Francesconi and her executive team; Gregg Popovich and the San Antonio Spurs; Bill Bartmann and CFS2; Alan Mulally and Ford; Jack Hauck, Larry Heitz, and Tubular Steel; and Matt Tomasic, Lynda Callon, and Chato Villalobos at the West Side Community Action Network Center in Kansas City.

The specifics of what these people and organizations did as they built their cultures are different. But one factor is constant, and this is what allowed all of them to get going in an outward-mindset way rather than be doomed to an inward mindset from the very beginning.

What is that constant? In each case, the leaders involved their organizations in pursuing a *collective result*—that is, a result that at once involved all the people in something much bigger than themselves *and* required that everyone join together with others in order for their efforts to succeed.

Chip Huth and his SWAT team together began reimagining what they owed to the members of the community, whether suspects or not. As a new collective vision emerged, the team began mobilizing together to interface with the community in ways that would create the relationship between police and the community that they had imagined. They became determined to show everyone unconditional respect. And this required that they treat each other as members of the team with that same respect.

Mark Ballif and Paul Hubbard worked with their employees to identify what they were trying to achieve. They built their culture by enabling others to apply their full creative energies to accomplish the collective result of *enriching a million lives every ten years, one person at a time.* Like Chip's SWAT team goal, this is a project that requires everyone; it requires them to enrich the lives of their clients and the lives of one another.

Gregg Popovich and the San Antonio Spurs—well, they are about championships. But their collective result informs how they pursue those championships. Winning a championship isn't yet the kind of objective that sets an organization up to work in an outward-mindset way, as chasing that dream can be done in inward-mindset ways as well. The collective result that motivates the Spurs has to do with a belief about how they must work together to win championships. They are committed to perfectly egoless teamwork. That is a result that requires everyone, together. Their results tell the story.

Bill Bartmann included his whole company in figuring out how to help the debtors they view as their clients. The best ideas for how to do this came from his team members rather than from him. Collectively they focus on raising up those in society who are struggling with debt. The entire company mobilizes around this objective.

Alan Mulally revitalized an almost-broken company by helping the team focus on making the best cars in the world, with profitable growth for all.[1] Their work needed to be beneficial to customers, suppliers, dealers, employees, and investors. That meant that all people had to step up and work together to help *everyone* benefit.

Jack Hauck, Larry Heitz, and the others at Tubular Steel mobilized to thrive in a rapidly declining market by empowering everyone in the organization to determine how each could positively impact profitability no matter his or her role. This project required everybody.

Matt Tomasic and his team engaged the day laborers on the West Side in the collective project of making the West Side a safe and clean place to live. This focus prompted them to take on projects in the community and also affected how the men looking for work acted in and interfaced with the community.

Louise Francesconi said this about the importance of a collective result in mobilizing her company's efforts to build an outward-mindset culture: "It is the focus on success—focusing on a result in a way that focuses on others—that is so accelerating. Culture moves around this. I don't care if some people are loud; I don't care if some people are quiet or whether they have good humor. We're not trying to have a homogenized group of people who work in the same way. Everybody works individually, but they work toward a collective solution. It's about taking difference and focusing together on results."

Every organization already exists as a collective. This is true whether one is speaking of an entire enterprise or a frontline team. Wherever people are organized together, a collective result already exists, just waiting to be named, collaborated around, and worked toward. However, very often, people in organizations mostly identify around their separate, individual roles. They don't have an understanding of how their own roles are essential to the overall collective result of the organization. Sometimes this is because the organization isn't explicitly organized around such a result. Other times this is because leaders haven't been clear enough or accountable enough to help their people see their impact on that result and take responsibility for making helpful adjustments.

Clarifying the collective result enables individuals and teams to improve their contributions within the organization without waiting for directives from those who have a broader view of the organization's interconnected parts. With this understanding, people don't require someone to align their roles relative to others; they can do this themselves. Imagine an organization of self-aligning individuals and teams who take responsibility for implementing the outward-mindset pattern, constantly adjusting what they do to ensure that their impact contributes to the accomplishment of the collective result. Every individual can decide to be this kind of contributor.

You may be wondering what you can do if you happen to work in an organization that isn't built around a collective result and you aren't in a position to do anything about that. Even in such a case, nothing is keeping you from defining your own role in terms of a collective result. We invite you to use the outward-mindset-at-work diagram (diagram 15) as a template to help you do this.

You are situated beneath a manager. What is your manager trying to achieve? The result your manager is trying to achieve is a collective result for you. Why? Because delivering your portion of your manager's result will require you to work collectively with others—with your customers, peers, and direct reports—to deliver the impact that your manager needs you to deliver.

DIAGRAM 15. **THE OUTWARD MINDSET AT WORK**

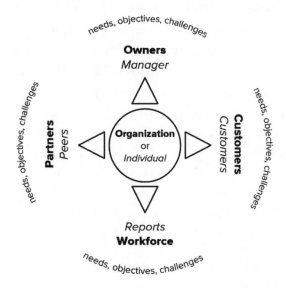

Here are some questions you can ask yourself as you utilize the outward-mindset-at-work framework for redefining your role in this way:

- *Toward your manager.* Do I have a clear understanding of my manager's objectives? What can I do to learn about them? What do I need to do to make sure that I am holding myself accountable for my contribution to my manager's results? Whom do I need to work with to ensure that I help my manager achieve those results?

- *Toward your customers.* Who are my customers, and what objectives do they have that I could help them with? How will I measure whether they are, in fact, helped by my efforts?
- *Toward your peers.* Which of my peers are affected by my work? Do I know whether I am helping or hindering them in their ability to accomplish their objectives?
- *Toward your direct reports.* Are my direct reports growing in their abilities? Have I worked with them to set a collective result for the entire team, and do they understand how they contribute to that result? Do they understand how their work impacts the ability of others to make their contributions to the collective result? And are they holding themselves accountable for that impact in each of the directions of their work? What can I do to help them to do this?

Wherever you are located in your organization, you can begin to rethink your work so that you see yourself in the context of achieving your own essential part of a collective result.

If you are a leader, you can do this for your own role and also work with your team or department to create the guiding framework that a collective result provides for the group.

If you are an executive, you have the opportunity to establish this vital foundation for outward-mindset working across your entire organization. Without a guiding result that requires all employees to pull together on behalf of others, outward-mindset cultures are difficult to sustain. With such an overarching collective result, however, you can take a series of concrete steps to successfully build an outward-mindset culture. We explore four of these in the next four chapters.

14. ALLOW PEOPLE TO BE FULLY RESPONSIBLE

Without realizing it, too many leaders assume that the role of leadership is to control. They espouse Plato's "division of labor," which, according to social thinker Hannah Arendt, has influenced government and military structures for thousands of years.[1] With the advent of the industrial revolution, she argues, corporate action, like the action of monarchies and armies, proceeded in two phases: planning and execution. Accordingly, in most organizations you find a class-divided lot: the minds and the bodies, the brains and the backs, the knowers and the doers, the manipulators and the manipulated.

Organizations that perpetuate this leader/led distinction tend to be riddled with justification and blame. Those who are tasked with *doing* can always blame poor performance on uninformed or unrealistic plans, while those who do the *planning* can always blame failures on poor execution. Leaders will cry for greater accountability, but the way most organizations are set up breeds a constant lack of accountability.

With an outward mindset, leaders position people to be fully responsible. This means that they empower their people with the responsibility both to execute *and* to plan their work. Consider an example of this in a home environment.

For years, John and Sylvia Harris had battled with their children over the family chores. Every week was the same story. The kids wouldn't do their basic chores, and the parents alternated between resentfully doing the work for them and living in an untidy home. As for enforcement, they vacillated between coming down hard on their children and disappointedly saying nothing. Everything they tried had exactly zero effect.

Then one day they realized that they had built their family approach to chores on the thinkers/doers distinction. When children are little, of course, parents need to do most of the thinking and planning. But John and Sylvia realized that they hadn't adjusted their approach much as their children had matured. The two of them still figured out what needed to be done and then told their children what their parts were in the grand family plan. The parents were the thinkers and the children were the doers.

With this realization, John and Sylvia adjusted their approach. *What would it be like if we brought the children into the planning process?* they wondered. Sylvia worried that the children might fail to see the importance of some of the tasks that she thought were essential. But, hoping for the best, she and John gathered the kids to figure out how they all thought family responsibilities should be handled—what those responsibilities should be, who should do them, when they needed and didn't need to be done, and so on.

In the midst of this discussion, the children wanted to think more broadly. "What about family fun?" one of them asked. "All we hear is 'do this' and 'do that.' Can we talk about the fun things we can do as a family too?"

And so the family talked together and planned together and disagreed together and compromised together. They learned about each other's needs—Mom's, Dad's, and each of the children's—which put them in a far better position to be able to think about the kinds of activities that could and should be done.

They planned their work and they planned their fun. They even planned the consequences for failing to do what they had mutually decided. And part of the planning, as urged by the children, was that not everything needed to be planned. Through this process, the "doers" became the "planners," and the "planners" joined the "doers." This change fueled a significant improvement in the accomplishment of tasks at home and the relationships within the family.

What was true in the Harris household is true of organizations generally. A distinguishing characteristic of organizations that operate with an outward mindset is the extent to which people in those organizations are allowed and encouraged to engage their whole brains in the planning as well as the doing of their work. By *whole brains*, we mean all of their faculties, including their wills and their hearts. People operating with an outward mindset exercise, as it were, their *whole selves*.

Now, you might be thinking, *if this worked for the Harris family, good for them. But that would never work in my family, or my company for that matter. My kids would take advantage of me if they had any say in what should happen at home, and the people at work rarely engage their brains in* doing *their work, let alone* planning *it.* Perhaps you've tried enlisting others in such a process and they simply didn't engage.

This is the situation that Dan Funk encountered as the new leader of a seriously dysfunctional healthcare facility his company had recently acquired. The employees of this facility were accustomed to fulfilling the mandates of the prior management team and seemed unresponsive to Dan's initial invitations to break free from their mindless, entrenched ways of working. So he called a meeting with the leadership team to attempt a reset.

"Okay," Dan began, "let's just brainstorm together. Imagine that there were no budget constraints here and no limitations. What have you always wanted to do for the patients here? What special services have you wished you could provide? What improvements have you wanted to make? The sky's the limit. Don't hold back. Just throw your ideas out there."

To Dan's surprise, no one said anything. He looked around at each member of the group, trying to coax out any responses.

Nothing.

Dan was perplexed. *How can no one have any ideas?* But then it dawned on him that the controlling, inwardly focused nature of the previous management had invited an inward focus in everyone in that facility. Rarely allowed the freedom to meet the needs that existed all around them, employees simply stopped seeing those needs. Seldom allowed to use their brains, they had stopped using them on behalf of the organization and its customers, the patients. It was as if the ability to see and respond to the needs and objectives of others was a muscle that, denied exercise, had atrophied and died.

So Dan tried a different tack. He began building relationships by working side-by-side with employees at every level in the facility, soliciting their ideas about how to improve this or that process as he engaged in the work with them. He carefully looked for opportunities to help people see possibilities for themselves. "What do you see that could be improved?" he asked as he worked. "What needs do your patients have? What might you do that would delight them?"

In this process, Dan actively had to resist the temptation to impose his own ideas. "I learned that when people came up with an idea, it was important to allow that idea to grow and be implemented. As long as an idea didn't take us backward or cause harm, the organization benefited more when the team members were allowed to implement their idea and discover how it could be improved than when I just tried to get them to implement my idea. I was constantly surprised by how many times I discovered that others' ideas turned out to be much better than mine and by the increased energy people brought to their work when they were empowered to implement their own ideas."

The joy these team members experienced when they saw the impact they could have on their coworkers and patients became contagious. Soon people throughout the facility were finding ways they could adjust their efforts to become more helpful and have greater impact.

Nevertheless, some employees were so numb to the needs around them that it appeared they would never be able to fully engage in helpful and productive ways. Dan recalls deciding early on that one employee in particular, a director of patient admissions, would simply not make it and would need to be fired. Dan remembers his surprise when she hesitantly approached him one day and shared with him that she had wanted to expand her responsibilities but was never given the opportunity. In addition to coordinating admissions, she asked if she could go to a tiny hospital close to her home to try to build relationships there. The hospital had never sent a patient to the facility, so with nothing to lose, Dan decided that this would be an opportunity to see what she was capable of.

"A month later," Dan recalls, "I was absolutely dumbfounded by the number of patients that began flooding into the facility as a result of her efforts." Dan has difficulty hiding his emotions as he relates this experience. "She saw a potential in herself that I had refused to see. Her life changed in profound ways because of this experience. But my life changed too. I resolved that I would never make assumptions about others' abilities before they are given appropriate opportunities. It sickens me to think about how many others I have left in my wake who could have been great but were never given the chance.

"I've realized," Dan concluded, "that when I try to impose my ideas on others and thereby refuse to allow them to think, I end up getting in the way more than I end up being helpful. It's not my job as a leader to have the solution to every problem. To those who bring you a problem they are facing, you have to be able to say, 'Hmm, that sounds like quite the conundrum. I look forward to hearing your best thinking about how we should fix that.' At the end of the day, my leadership effectiveness is measured not by what *I* am able to accomplish but by what those whom I lead are able to accomplish."

Rob Anderson, CEO of Superior Water and Air, a large heating and air business, gathered his leadership team to begin applying the whole-brain or whole-self approach of an outward mindset in their company. As part of this effort, they reconsidered their work with the company's customer service reps (CSRs). "If we started by thinking about the CSRs' needs and challenges and objectives," Rob asked, "what might occur to us?"

"Well, to begin with," one of his executives answered, "we'd start learning their names." The others in the room nodded and spontaneously started trying to name as many of the customer service reps as they could.

"And we'd want to learn more about what it's like to do their jobs," another remarked. "We should probably join them and try to do what we've asked them to do—to see how we'd like it."

"I tried that one morning," one of them said. "I couldn't get out of there fast enough. I could never do that job!"

"And yet they make far less money than we do," another chimed in. This comment got everyone thinking.

"So what *would* it be like to be a CSR?" Rob asked. The group discussed the realities of the CSRs' job—from their less-than-ideal work setting to the pressures of dealing with customer complaints to the demands made on them by various departments in the company.

"You know," one of the executives said, "we've really set things up backward. We just told them what they need to do and the results they need to deliver. No wonder the job is a drag."

At this point, one of the executives leveled a critique toward this whole line of thinking. "So what are we supposed to do then," he asked, "just let them do what they want to do? We *need* them to accomplish the goals we've set for them. Our results depend on it."

This objection sounds compelling. But it rests on the assumption that others can't be trusted to accomplish anything unless they are told what they need to accomplish and how they need to accomplish it. This is the same thinker/doer distinction that the Harris family had to abandon before they could make real improvements in their family and that could have squashed the potential of Dan Funk's admissions director.

People should be involved in determining the results they need to deliver in the context of a collective result. Everyone has a brain, and everyone in an organization should be encouraged to engage and use that brain to think about and execute his or her role. After rethinking their approach toward the CSRs by utilizing the outward-mindset pattern, Rob and his colleagues had to resist the temptation to rethink the CSRs' role for them. To be effective in their leadership, Rob and his team needed to help the customer service reps engage in the same process themselves—to take responsibility for rethinking their roles by using the outward-mindset pattern from chapter 9, which is reproduced in diagram 16.

DIAGRAM 16. **THE OUTWARD-MINDSET PATTERN FOR AN INDIVIDUAL**

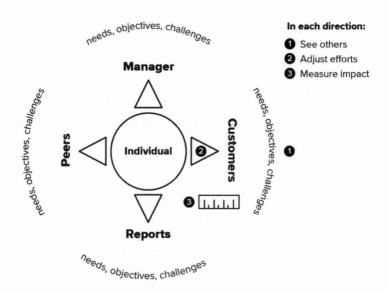

Applying the outward-mindset pattern, the CSRs should learn about the objectives of those they impact, *including* the executive team. They would then be able to use their own creativity and initiative to determine what adjustments they should make to become more helpful in their role. They would then measure the impact of their efforts in each direction and on the organization as a whole.

One of the reasons the outward-mindset approach can be scaled so readily by people up, down, and across an organization is that outward-mindset work at the individual level mirrors the same work for a team and an entire organization or enterprise. Diagram 17 shows the same framework with enterprise-level categories in each of the four directions of the diagram.

Compare diagrams 16 and 17. Individual workers and the enterprise as a whole both have customers. Both have those they report to—a manager in the case of an individual, and a board, shareholders, or others for the enterprise. Both have peers or partners (at the enterprise level, partners might include suppliers). And all managers in an organization have those who report to them, just as an enterprise has responsibility for the workforce as a whole.

DIAGRAM 17. **THE OUTWARD-MINDSET PATTERN FOR AN ORGANIZATION**

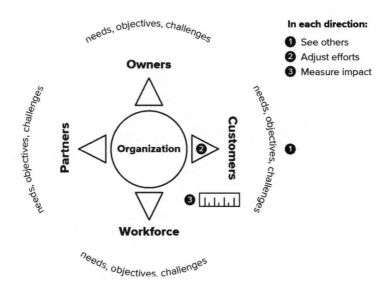

Because the outward-mindset approach is identical whether working at the individual, team, or enterprise level, an organization's leaders can rethink the organization's work at the enterprise level in exactly the same way that all the employees in the organization will be rethinking and aligning their work in their individual roles.

A way to make this scaled alignment explicit is to help each person, each team, each department or division, and the enterprise as a whole construct their own outward-mindset-at-work diagrams. Imagine an organization composed of individuals and teams with complete clarity and transparency about whom they have responsibilities toward. Imagine that they are committed to doing what they do in ways that help those they have responsibilities toward succeed in their efforts. Imagine that all the parts of the organization are supplied with the understanding and tools to operate in an outwardly focused way. And imagine that the enterprise itself—from mission and strategy to structure and systems—was rethought in this way so that the entire organization was mobilized for maximal impact.

Imagine as well that you could look over the expanse of the organization and see where the efforts of individuals and teams were focused inward so that you could determine where to begin putting more of your time and attention. And imagine that you could help all people in the organization become self-managing and self-accountable in each direction of their work, continuously and energetically adjusting their efforts to be more helpful. What would happen to the productivity of your organization if you could invite an outward mindset to that degree?

15. SHRINK DISTINCTIONS

One of the ways the leader/led distinction we discussed in chapter 14 shows up is through what we call *trappings of difference*—that is, outward manifestations of status that only the preferred can enjoy. When our mindsets are inward, we see no problem with such distinctions; they likely seem well deserved. In contrast, when our mindsets are outward, we see that others matter like we ourselves matter. We possess the characteristic that Mark Ballif and Paul Hubbard, whom we discussed in chapter 1, identified from their experience to be the most important leadership essential: humility. We understand that any practice or policy that communicates to others that they don't really matter like we do can end up creating barriers to building an outward organization.

On a client engagement in London, two of our Arbinger consultants stepped into the elevator on their first visit to a client's headquarters and pushed the button for the building's top floor. A man in the lift said, "Ah, top floor." A hint of resentment in his voice clearly communicated what he didn't say: *So you think you're big shots, huh?* The man's comment suggested that one sticking point at this company might be the way company leadership had chosen to segregate themselves from others in the company.

In some cases, there may be good business reasons why the executives need to have offices together and apart from others in the company. But even in such cases, it still leaves open the question of why they would need to be together on the best floor of the building. Why not a middle floor? Or why not the basement level? Leaders who question the trappings of privilege that they enjoy, and, where strong business reasons for maintaining the differences don't exist, are willing to collapse the distinctions between themselves and others in the company, create an environment where mindset change is significantly more likely to succeed.

The same is true in every environment. A mother who applies one set of rules to herself and another set to her children, for example, undercuts her ability to influence positive mindset change in her children. Why? Because the more lenient set of rules for the parent communicates that the mother thinks she is more important than her children, which invites resistance and even resentment toward her and her rules. Parents will have more success with their children if they live by the same set of rules as their children.

Of course, there are differences between parents and children—between their responsibilities, and so on—so there will always be differences in some of their activities. The same can be said about workplaces. The CEO has a different set of responsibilities than the newly hired college graduate, so no one would expect that everything in the workplace would be the same for the two of them. However, CEOs and other leaders who minimize the privileges they enjoy compared to their people inspire far greater levels of devotion than those who love their privileges.

This was one of the major reasons why Alan Mulally, whom we discussed in chapter 9, was able to lead such positive change, first at Boeing and then at Ford. Mulally was beloved by workers at all levels in part because he collapsed the trappings of difference. He didn't present himself as a big shot. Instead of eating lunch in Ford's opulent executive dining room, for example, he ate lunch in the company cafeteria, taking a plastic tray just like the next person and working his way down the line. He was as interested in listening to and learning from the man on the assembly line as he was the person next to him at the executive team meeting. He felt no need or desire to separate himself from his coworkers simply because the organization chart said he was at the top.

A good rule of thumb is that an organization is ready to deploy mindset-change efforts to the next level in an organization when those in the next level are seeing real change in the level above. Leaders demonstrate noticeable change as they begin questioning the privileges they reserve for themselves. To prompt such helpful changes, leaders could begin asking themselves questions like these: Do we need the prime parking spots? The best office spaces? Do we segregate ourselves in different cafeterias or more preferred parts of the building? Can perks that the few enjoy be made available to others? Can any trappings of "bigshotness" be removed? If we treat and pay ourselves generously, are we appropriately generous as well with our employees? And so on.

As we learned in chapters 9 and 10, the methodology for turning from an inward mindset to an outward mindset is to apply the outward-mindset pattern. This pattern can guide you as you question the traditions and practices in your organization. You could begin by allowing yourself to be guided by questions that prompt a careful consideration of the experience of others throughout the organization: What is it like to be an employee here? Do employees feel valued? Do they feel understood? Do they feel that the leadership appreciates them? What distinctions in the workplace might be troubling to them? What distinctions might make them feel less important?

Then ask questions that might spark ideas about what adjustments might be helpful: What can we do to help others understand how we value and appreciate them? What can we do to more fully understand others' viewpoints and concerns? What trappings of leadership currently exist in the organization? Which of these trappings and differences make good business sense and which do not? What can we do to collapse distinctions between leaders and others in the organization?

Lastly, consider how you will measure the impact of these changes and continuously reassess the distinctions that arise: What can we do to stay more fully connected to employees? What can we do to ensure that we collect and stay open to feedback and suggestions from people at all levels of the organization? How can we continuously check ourselves as leaders to make sure that we are not letting unnecessary distinctions separate us from others?

A number of years ago, Scott O'Neil, who led the sports division of Madison Square Garden (MSG) at the time and who now leads the Philadelphia 76ers, asked us to work with his leaders. One of our colleagues met with Scott and his leadership team in New York. A couple of hours into the session, the team considered a question about differences that sparked a deeply important set of discoveries: Which people or groups of people in this organization probably most feel as if they are seen as objects?

As the team listed the candidate groups, they were troubled by the realization that the people at MSG who probably most feel as if they are seen as objects are the people in the organization who most touch their customers: the ticket takers and the ushers at Madison Square Garden. The team thought those groups probably felt ignored, underappreciated, and taken for granted. And this suddenly worried them. If those in the organization who interact with the customers are themselves seen and treated as objects, how are they likely to see and treat the customers? The leaders began thinking about what they could do to collapse distinctions in the ways their frontline people were treated as compared to others in the organization.

MSG leadership began to make concerted efforts to learn the names and backgrounds of the part-time game-day employees. They figured that these people were as valuable to the organization as the season-ticket holders and sponsors and that the attitudes and actions of the leadership and full-time staff should communicate that. They didn't think that anyone should feel that he or she was above doing what the part-time staff was being asked to do. "If you see a piece of paper on the ground, pick it up" became a running mantra for MSG leadership and full-time employees. It was one way to collapse distinctions. As a result of these and other initiatives, a we-are-in-this-together mentality spread throughout the organization.

A healthcare client that operates many hospitals discovered this same issue within its organization. The people in its emergency rooms who most feel as if they are seen as objects are those who first meet with the patients and who shape the patients' initial experience. These are the people at the desk who check patients in, take care of all the insurance issues, and so on. Revealingly, this category of workers is known in the medical industry as *ancillary staff*. Think about this term and what it communicates: *ancillary*.

When the doctors, nurses, and technicians considered what these employees likely assumed about their role given their title, they intuited the same truth that those at Madison Square Garden did: the patient experience in their hospitals could be no better than the experience of those they thought of as ancillary staff. Like the leaders at Madison Square Garden, these leaders began to rethink the differences in their workplaces.

Richard Sheridan and his colleagues at the brilliant software design firm Menlo Innovations are fantastic at many things, including collapsing distinctions. All the employees at Menlo, including Rich, work together in a single-space environment. Everyone's desk is the same. The company holds small-group and large-group meetings in this same environment, where everyone can listen in, learn, and participate.

"Some may wonder," Rich says, "where, in a wide-open, no-rules space, the CEO sits. Most companies mark the status of their high-level managers by gifting them suites. But our C-suite isn't a corner office; it's a table out in the middle of the space, with an old white Apple iMac, notable because it may be the slowest computer in the entire company. That's where I, as the CEO, sit." He adds, "I sit out in the middle of the room because that's where the team has put me. Sometimes the team decides I need to be closer to the action, where I can overhear more of the details of a particularly challenging project. When that is the case, they move my table right into the mix of that project's pod of tables and people. Every few months I have to adjust my walking pattern to a new desk location."[1]

Rich and his team have even collapsed the trappings of the company as a whole. If you want to visit Menlo, you park in a garage between Washington and Liberty Streets in Ann Arbor,

Michigan, and take the elevator to the basement. There, in a windowless cave that was once a food court and mall in the basement of a seven-story parking structure, you will find this wildly successful no-big-shots-allowed company.

When leaders begin to take seriously the project of not taking themselves too seriously and begin collapsing the distinctions between themselves and others, they are positioned to begin scaling mindset change.

16. TURN SYSTEMS OUTWARD

An important aspect of leading successful mindset change is a willingness to reconsider the objectives, systems, policies, and processes of an organization. Systems and processes that are designed to manage objects rather than empower people have widespread negative consequences. Efforts to rethink those systems and processes from an outward-mindset perspective can deliver huge benefits.

Recall the story of the Harris family in chapter 14. The fundamental change in their planning process resulted in a significant improvement in the helping at home and in the relationships within the family. This didn't solve all their problems, even around chores, but it established an entirely different foundation upon which to handle failures as well as successes. The Harrises' new approach turned their family planning into an outward-mindset process, which inspired, reinforced, and supported outward-mindset working.

By contrast, if an organization tells its people to operate with an outward mindset but persists in implementing systems and processes that are designed to "manage" objects, the systems and processes will end up winning, and the organization and its customers, employees, and stakeholders will end up losing.

Consider, for example, the effect of a forced-distribution or bell-curve ranking system, where employees are compared to each other to determine their futures. A new manager in an internationally dispersed security team within a PC tech giant began to see real progress in helping his team members develop an outward mindset despite the geographical distance and absence of significant face-to-face interaction. Team members had begun to adjust their work to take into account the needs of their coworkers in an effort to deliver their services to internal customer departments around the world.

As the end of the year approached, however, this leader began to notice team members reverting back to their old inward-mindset behaviors. They started hoarding information and stopped collaborating. They began pushing their own task-oriented agendas, regardless of the difficulties they created for their coworkers.

In his frustration, the leader picked up the phone and called team members from Japan to Johannesburg to ask why attitudes were sliding backward. Some employees were defensive, excusing their inward-mindset behaviors by blaming their colleagues. Others were evasive, denying that any change had occurred. Finally, one of his team members told him the truth. "Don't you know?" this employee asked. "It's the end of the year and time for performance reviews. We all know how this works. You have to rate the members of the team, and very few of us will make it into the top 15 percent and get a bonus. And the bottom 10 percent will be getting sacked. How did you think we would behave given what's coming?"

Despite the almost irresistible temptation toward an inward mindset that such a system invites, some companies that see their people as objects have difficulty seeing viable alternatives to such a system. A bell curve forces performance ratings based on the relative performance of team members against each other. It does not rate the actual productivity and results of team members. A true review of performance based on results relative to opportunity for impact might suggest that far more than 10 percent of employees need to go or, on the other hand, that every single member of a team should stay. But this would require that organizations, instead of managing through mandates, entrust their leaders and managers with actually leading and growing their people.

We are sympathetic to why organizations, particularly very large ones, sometimes feel compelled to adopt a forced-distribution approach. When managers are asked to rate their employees, they often feel pressure to inflate their ratings. Sometimes managers do this because, from an inward mindset, they have a need for their people to like them. Other times they may not have taken their leadership responsibilities seriously enough to know where their people need to improve. Whatever the reasons may be for the rating inflation, organizations have mandated forced-distribution approaches to force managers to rank order their people. This comes at a huge organizational cost, as we have discussed, but it is understandable why some organizations nevertheless have made that choice.

If you find yourself working within such a forced-distribution system, with no authority to change it, does that mean that you are stuck? Consider how you still could operate within that system with an outward mindset and help your people to do the same. For example, what if you gathered your team and taught them about the outward-mindset-at-work framework and the outward-mindset pattern? You could encourage them to hold themselves accountable for their impact in each of the four directions of their work, and you could let them know that their annual performance rating will reflect their efforts to hold themselves accountable in this way. You could then meet with them on a regular basis to see how they are doing. Meeting regularly with them, you would be positioned to help them improve their work and increase their level of self-accountability.

Your efforts with your people wouldn't be able to rescue the whole system from the perverse effects of the forced-distribution approach. However, you will have been able to help your people, within that system, to grow in productive ways. No system can keep you from doing that, unless you allow it to.

That being said, if your organization tells you to have an outward mindset but rewards and pays you for being inward, the perverse incentives can seem overwhelming. Some of the most common structural impediments to outward-mindset working are inwardly focused success metrics.

As a case in point, consider the story of Tom Brakins—affectionately called Brak by those close to him. Brak is a top sales leader in one of the most powerful companies in the world, a company we will call Landa Corporation. He was commissioned by his company to try to rescue one of its most important business accounts. By the time Brak took over the account, Landa had fallen to number sixteen (and last) on the client's preferred-supplier list. His contact at the client informed him that Landa would be off the list next time around. This meant that Brak's company was in real danger of losing an account worth more than $50 million.

Brak handpicked a team to help him on the account, and they threw themselves into helping the customer. Within eighteen months, Landa had climbed to the number-one spot on the same list—an impossible, unheard-of jump. The company had gone from worst to first in eighteen months because the client felt that Brak and his team had the client's back.

Soon thereafter, Brak's counterpart at the client, whom we will call Julie, sent Brak and his wife a thoughtful care package to congratulate them on the birth of their child. She followed this up with a kind voice-mail message in which she referenced the upcoming renewal of her company's contract with Landa. She told Brak that they could save the energies of their respective teams before the holidays if she and Brak met one-on-one and got the deal done by early December. She told him that she had the budget and that in her mind this was going to be easy.

This was tremendous news to Brak for a few reasons. First, Julie's words reinforced the level of trust she had in his team and Landa's services. Second, with the scope of this deal, Brak and his team would hit their numbers, which would be important for the company as a whole. And third, for a reason peculiar to Landa, the timely close would mean that they would meet the requirements of an internal Landa metric that lay like a sharp blade on the necks of the company's sales teams.

What is this metric that stirs such fear among Landa's salespeople? A large portion of Landa's revenues come from existing customer contracts with built-in renewal dates. Someone in the finance area of the company had researched these accounts and found that renewals that were closed after their renewal dates resulted on average in significantly reduced contract amounts. Company leaders wanted to force their salespeople to get the deals done before the renewal date passed, and this renewal metric was their way to do that. To hit the metric, salespeople must close all such contracts by the renewal date at 105 percent or more of the prior contract amount. Failure to do this means a huge hit to compensation up and down the line.

So much for the theory; here is what happens in actual practice: The penalties for missing the metric are so severe that salespeople end up granting concessions they wouldn't give otherwise to close their deals on time and achieve the metric. So a metric designed to keep salespeople from losing too much after the renewal date actually incentivizes them to give away too much in advance of the renewal date. Like many internal metrics, a measure that seems to make sense in the abstract produces tremendously negative unintended consequences when put into actual practice.

In Brak's case, the contract renewal date with Julie's company was December 31. He and Julie worked out a $66 million renewal contract by early December. This figure represented a nearly $10 million discount off the normal value of the services Landa would be providing. But Brak felt these discounts both helped Julie and her company and made good business sense for Landa as well. He and his team were glad that the deal was being finalized far enough in advance of the metric's deadline to avoid the pressure that builds when the clock is winding down.

Then things got rocky. Julie's finance person ran the numbers on the deal and thought they showed that Landa was taking advantage of them. At first, Julie didn't believe this, as it flew in the face of her experience with Brak and his team. But her analyst was adamant, and he convinced Julie that Landa wasn't being truthful. She felt betrayed and jumped into the details to see how Brak and his team were stiffing them.

Brak was sure that Julie's finance person had fouled up the analytics, as Landa's own calculations showed that Julie's company was getting just as good of a deal as Brak had outlined. The effect of this delay, however, was that the December 31 deadline of Landa's own internal metric started to cut at the psyches of those up and down Landa's leadership chain. They started worrying about themselves rather than the customer. Brak was getting severe pressure to do anything necessary to get the deal done by December 31.

Feeling anxious himself, Brak gave in. To ensure that he and his team would meet their metric, he ended up approving an additional $6 million in cuts to lower the contract to $60 million.

You might think that this was good for the customer. In fact, however, these cuts weren't being made for the benefit of the customer, and both Brak's and Julie's team members knew this. The whole machinery within Landa was grinding to meet its own metric. While it's true that Julie's company happened to receive further financial benefit as a result of this, Landa's inward focus turned a relationship-based, outward-mindset approach into a transaction-based sale, which would put at risk Landa's ability to help Julie and her team in the future.

Then the situation got worse. Julie suddenly dropped off the grid. Days slipped by without the deal getting signed, and Brak couldn't get ahold of her. He even flew into town unannounced to try to meet with her, but to no avail. Panic set in among Landa's North American business unit leadership team. If this deal Brak was working on missed the metric, it would put the whole North American number below plan. Careers hung in the balance.

Finally, on December 28, Julie called Brak. It turns out that a deal of this size could be signed only by her company's CEO, and Julie had been unable or unwilling to take the deal up the line for his signature. By now the CEO was out of the country and wouldn't be available to sign until the first or second week of January. "That's not going to work, Julie," Brak responded. "The concessions we made were contingent on your company executing the deal by the thirty-first. January isn't going to work for us."

"Sorry," Julie said, "but that's the best I can do. It's going to have to be January."

Brak was overcome with disappointment—mostly in himself, as he knew that allowing himself to be driven by a metric that had nothing to do with the customer had undermined his relationship with the customer.

They closed the deal two weeks later at $60 million and missed the internal metric. As a result, North America missed its number, which had serious repercussions. Furthermore, despite the huge discounts received, the customer specifically demanded that Tom Brakins be removed from the account. And with Brak off the account, Landa immediately began tumbling down the client's preferred-supplier list again.

Even today, you hear the pain in Brak's voice as he speaks of this experience. "All of this could have been managed, if not avoided altogether," he said, "had we thought more about our customer and *their* metrics and less about ourselves and our own screwed-up inward metric. Our inward focus messed us up both internally and externally: externally because this whole experience ruined the relationship with this customer, and internally because about twenty people inside Landa lost their heart for the organization because of what happened on this deal. They heard all the internal messaging—'Obsess about the customer, obsess about the customer'—and then, when it came right down to it, they saw company leadership, including me, obsessing only about ourselves. From that moment on, a whole bunch of people basically quit on the company. They didn't believe in the place anymore."

What went wrong in this case? The metric Landa's leadership devised to manage the efforts of their salespeople had no connection whatsoever to the needs of customers. As a result, the metric turned the salespeople's minds away from their customers and toward themselves. Obsession with the internal metric without a counterbalancing focus on the needs of the customer rewarded and invited an inward mindset.

Compare this story with the story of Hope Arising in chapter 10. Hope Arising discovered that measuring success in terms of how much clean water they delivered (an internal metric) did not yet tell them whether they were meeting the needs of the people they were trying to serve. Becoming more curious about the people they were serving, they discovered that those people cared about clean water primarily because they wanted their children to be in school. After discovering this, Hope Arising began measuring the success of its efforts by measuring the days spent in school by the children in those areas. Note how different this focus feels from the focus Landa invites from its salespeople. Whereas Landa measures success primarily in terms of the revenue it receives from its customers, Hope Arising measures success primarily in terms of the positive impact it is having on its customers.

Which organization would you rather work for?

Which organization would you rather buy from?

Leaders of organizations that operate with an inward mindset may feel confused by what they see in organizations that operate with an outward mindset. It will seem risky to manage those they see and treat as objects with systems and processes that are designed to empower people.

This is one of the reasons why an outward-mindset approach becomes such a competitive advantage. Those who are unwilling to adopt an outward mindset won't be able to successfully replicate outward-mindset systems, processes, and approaches, while organizations that turn systems and processes outward become positioned to achieve and sustain higher levels of performance. Consider a few examples from earlier chapters.

The outward-mindset planning process adopted by Louise Francesconi and her executive team (chapter 4) allowed them to dramatically shorten the planning cycle as compared to their competitors. The outward-mindset customer service processes and employee incentive structures at CFS2 (chapter 8) produced industry-leading returns. The outward-mindset reporting practices at Ford (chapter 9) positioned the company to be able to get in front of the financial crisis in ways that others couldn't. Tubular Steel's disciplined effort to help every person and every team in the organization to rethink their roles and responsibilities in an outward-mindset way produced industry-leading performance (chapter 11).

Hiring and onboarding approaches, sales and marketing processes, budgeting practices, incentive structures, performance evaluation and management systems, and every other organizational system, structure, and process can be conceived and deployed in inward-mindset or outward-mindset ways. Organizations that are serious about operating with an outward mindset turn these systems and processes outward to invite and reinforce outward-mindset working.

17. IMPLEMENT A GAME PLAN

Everyone knows how to ride a bike. Right? But how about a bike that's backward? How well do you think you could ride a bike that turns right when you steer to the left and turns left when you steer to the right? As a bit of a prank, a group of welders rigged up such a bike and then challenged their engineer colleague, Destin Sandlin, to ride it.

Destin is the wide-eyed, enthusiastic creator of educational discovery videos on a YouTube channel called Smarter Every Day. The video he produced about his adventure trying to ride this bike went viral and is Smarter Every Day's most popular video, with over 20 million views to date.

But back to the bike. How hard could it be? Seriously.

As it turns out, *very*.

No one has ever been able to successfully ride the bike, at least not right away. Destin has tested this around the world, offering $200 to anyone who can ride the bike just ten feet. He still has that $200.

But Destin's an engineer—he's methodical, and he perseveres. He practiced riding the bike for eight straight months. Every day, he'd go out to his driveway for five minutes and give it a go. We're not sure how he arrived at the formula of five minutes a day; maybe that's all the falling off that he could take in the early stages. In any case, he devoted five minutes to it every day, and every day he had the same experience: wobbling, faltering, and falling off.

How much failure can a person take? It would have been easy for Destin to quit. But he didn't quit. He kept getting back on the bike. He kept trying.

Then, one day, eight months after he had started working on it, something clicked. One moment he couldn't ride the bike, but the next moment he could. The short but regular practice sessions had, over time, rewired his brain and developed in him a new kind of muscle memory. He could ride a backward bike. He could ride it fast, and he could ride it smoothly. He had proved it could be done, so he thought that his experiment was over.

But then he thought of a second experiment. He now could ride a backward bicycle, but after all that time learning how to do it, could he still ride a normal one?

While in Amsterdam, the "city of bikes," Destin scheduled a meet-up with someone who would bring a bike for him to try. A few Dutch onlookers watched as the dumb American couldn't peddle a normal bike more than two feet before jerking to a stop. This struggle continued for twenty exasperating minutes. Destin was dumbfounded. He had ridden a bike from the time he was a small child; it was completely second nature to him. And yet he could no longer do it. He had educated all his impulses to suc-cessfully steer a backward bike. The normal bike now seemed backward to him.

Then, just as something had clicked after months of practice that allowed him to ride a backward bike, something clicked once more, and he was able to tap into all his experience riding a normal bike. He could ride it again. All the people watching thought the whole thing was a stunt. Who can't ride a bike, after all? But they didn't know how Destin had unlearned how to ride a normal bike by teaching himself to ride a backward one.

Let's think about what these bike-riding experiments might suggest about mindset change. What if you have spent much of your life with an inward mindset? What if you've been inward a lot at home and quite often at work as well? And what if inward-mindset practices and patterns have predominated at your workplace for years? What if you've had a lot of company in the inward-mindset box?

If this has been your reality, how easy should you expect it to be to shift to an outward mindset?

We would suggest that, like riding a backward bike, you should expect that attempts to shift to an outward mindset would seem backward at first. You should expect to falter, to wobble, to fall off. But here are three pieces of good news. The first is that, unlike Destin, you've actually had experience riding the kind of bike you're trying to master. You're already riding an outward-mindset bike, if you will, in many situations in your life. So learning to ride that bike in new situations isn't so much learning a new skill from scratch as it is learning how to implement what you already know how to do in situations where it is more difficult for you.

The second piece of good news is that, as was the case with Destin, you don't have to try to ride the new bike all the time. It is enough to do a little at a time and just keep practicing it. You should expect new attempts at mindset change to feel unnatural and awkward at first. You should expect to fall off. The question that matters is, Will you climb back on for five minutes the next day? And the day after that? Devoting consistent effort over an extended period is how you build new muscle memory not only in your body but also in your soul. This piece of good news comes with a corollary: unlike a bike, you don't just put away your mindset after you've finished practicing. Every effort to live or work with an outward mindset has lingering effects. The five minutes you spend consciously applying outward-mindset tools and strategies will position you to be more outward than you otherwise might have been over the rest of your day.

Which brings us to the third piece of good news. The better one gets at riding the new bike, the more natural and instinctual that form of riding becomes. What had seemed backward at first ends up feeling natural, and old habits no longer hold power over us. So if you have struggled with an inward mindset in different aspects of your life, realize that learning to take on an outward mindset is more than simply learning a different way; it's actually the way one expunges the old way. Outwardness does to inwardness what light does to darkness: it chases it away.

In our work with clients over more than three decades, we have learned the importance of regular practice. Individuals and organizations turn from an inward mindset to an outward mindset by committing to take small but consistent actions over time.

A manager who wants her team to exhibit more of an outward mindset can lead that effort by building with them an implementation plan of consistent outward-mindset strategies and actions. For example, given that lateral awareness is a key indicator of mindset (as discussed in chapter 10), the team might decide to devote five minutes of every team meeting to building lateral awareness among team members. They might also deploy a strategy for building lateral awareness about the needs, objectives, and challenges of other teams in the company. They might work on ways they could measure their impact on each other and on other teams (as also discussed in chapter 10). Or they might decide to always apply the outward-mindset pattern—SAM—to team and business issues they are tackling or to turn each of their objectives outward the way Al Klein's marketing team did toward the sales team, as discussed in chapter 11. The team could decide to spend a few minutes in successive team meetings gaining clarity around the team's collective goal and how it nests into the organization's collective goal, as discussed in chapter 13, or to work on shrinking distinctions, as discussed in chapter 15, or turning team systems and processes outward, as discussed in chapter 16. Or they could decide simply to study the outward mindset for a few minutes together on a regular basis and let those discussions guide real-time implementation of outward-mindset principles. And so on.

Which particular outward-mindset strategies one begins to deploy is not as important as simply beginning to implement any outward-mindset strategy. Start where you are. Do a little at a time. Keep at it. Don't quit riding the bike when you start feeling wobbly. It's okay to put it away, but just take it out to the driveway again the next day. Five minutes a day. That's the game plan. If you keep after it, individually and collectively, you'll experience the shift. Today, outward-mindset approaches might not seem natural to you, but eventually they will. And you and your team will find it increasingly difficult to act in any other way.

18. THE ROAD AHEAD

Near the end of an Arbinger training event with employees of a large manufacturing company, the facilitator explained that one person changing to an outward mindset doesn't *make* others respond in kind; others still choose their own mindsets.

One of the participants spoke up. "I understand that," she said, "but I often respond differently to people that I know care about me; I just do. They don't *make* me respond differently, but it's almost like I can't help it. Something about their concern for me invites me to start thinking more carefully about them." Heads nodded around the room.

"That's my experience too," said another. "For me, it's surprising how often mindset change in one person *does* end up inviting change in others."

A man sitting in the back of the room strenuously objected. "I don't agree with that at all," he argued, his voice rising. "I'm outward mindset almost all the time, but it doesn't seem to matter!" The veins in his neck bulged as he said this, and some participants chuckled to themselves at the apparent irony in his response.

At this point, a woman in the back of the room raised her hand. She hadn't spoken in the group until this moment. "Can I tell you a story?" she asked.

"Certainly, please," the facilitator responded.

She began:

Many years ago, my brother committed a terrible crime that landed my family on the front page of the newspapers for months. The ordeal destroyed our reputation and ripped at the fabric of our family. There is no way that I can describe the confusion and pain we all felt; it devastated us. One by one we moved away from the area to get out from beneath the shame we felt and to try to build new lives. As the years went on, we would periodically gather for a few days to keep the family connected, but the new family fabric we were fashioning was knit partly through the collective act of exorcising our brother from our family identity.

After a few decades, this older brother was finally released from prison. It had been almost long enough for us to completely expunge him from our consciousness. Yet suddenly he was back. Soon thereafter, we happened to have a family gathering scheduled, and he showed up. We made small talk with him, but there was strain and discomfort in every word. How could there not have been? Here was the guy we still felt had ruined us.

After a short pause, she continued.

Sometime during lunch on that first day, my brother slid away. By evening time, we suspected that he would not be returning, and to be honest, we were relieved. We didn't have to force conversations anymore; we could just relax and enjoy each other. We could go back to being the family we had finally managed to become.

As the evening progressed, however, a realization settled on me. I saw how close we were to losing this brother
again—this time maybe forever. And I knew in that
moment that I couldn't allow this to happen. That didn't
mean I no longer had hard feelings or anything; I was as
conflicted as the rest of the family. It just meant that I knew
I couldn't just let him go—like I didn't care about him or
something. I resolved in that moment that I would maintain the family's connection with him by reaching out to
him with a letter every month. It was a small thing, but it
was something I knew I could do.

That was seven years ago, and I've written him every
month since. And you know something? I've yet to hear
back from him.

There was an audible gasp in the room. "No, but that's okay,"
she responded. "Because I'm not doing it for me, I'm doing it
for him."

This story illustrates critical lessons for anyone who wants
to sustain an outward mindset. Sometimes having an outward
mindset is rather easy. We may be among people who care about
each other, and it may seem utterly natural and easy to respond
to them with an outward mindset. Our teams at work, for example, may be filled with energetic and helpful individuals. Or we
may be fortunate to be in a family filled with kind and generous
people. In such cases it is relatively easy to maintain an outward
mindset. Why? Because we feel so cared for and considered by
those whose mindsets are outward toward us that we feel no
need or desire to be defensive toward them. Almost effortlessly

we find ourselves naturally showing consideration in return. As Brenda Ueland, whom we quoted in chapter 10, taught, we find ourselves *unfolding* in the presence of such people. An outward mindset in one person invites the same in others.

Unfortunately, the same principle works as well in reverse. When we interact with someone who is operating with an inward mindset, we may feel that he is failing to consider our views or opinions, and we can see that as an invitation to take offense or withdraw. If we do, we will give back to this person exactly what he is giving to us, and we will become embroiled in an inward-mindset struggle like the credit and sales teams we discussed in chapter 11. Such struggles may last for a minute, for a day, or perhaps even for a lifetime.

Although an inward mindset in one person does not *cause* others to respond with an inward mindset, it does *invite* others to respond in kind. The challenge is how to respond with an outward mindset when those we work or live with invite the opposite.

Long before Mark Ballif, whom we wrote about in chapter 1, became a successful executive, he was a young worker in his first postcollege job and was struggling with his boss. He had graduated feeling as if he had a lot to contribute, and he elected to join a young company with a mission he really believed in. One of the first dozen employees at the firm, he was excited to help the organization grow into what he knew it could become.

However, as the days grew into months, and those months expanded into the first two years of his professional career, Mark grew increasingly disenchanted. Two years in, he felt as if he had no more responsibility in the organization than on the day he started—which meant one thing: his boss didn't think he had any more to offer.

Mark felt held back, overlooked, and unappreciated. Every day he felt victimized—prohibited from exercising his gifts. Frustration grew into anger. The future Mark had envisioned seemed forever out of reach. He started to circulate his résumé.

He was in the middle of planning his exit when his boss's boss, someone Mark looked to as a mentor, said that he wanted to meet with him. After all those months, Mark finally felt vindicated. *He sees how much I'm giving here,* Mark thought. *He knows how hard it is to work for my boss, so he's going to step in and make things right. He's going to console me, tell me I'm doing okay, and then help chart a pathway for me to grow in the company.* Mark walked into the meeting with hopeful expectation.

When he sat down, however, his mentor said, "Mark, we need more from you."

Mark was mortified. This assessment was so different from what he had anticipated that it stunned him into silence. He listened as his mentor tried to open Mark's eyes to how Mark had been holding back from giving his best in his work.

Mark tried to defend himself in that meeting, but the conversation led him to begin rethinking some of his actions. He went home and couldn't sleep that night.

As he lay in bed, Mark replayed in his mind many events from the prior couple of years. At first, these memories rekindled his anger. But as he reconsidered what his mentor had said to him, he began to notice truths about his experience that he had previously overlooked. He saw himself avoiding his boss and openly criticizing what she wanted done. He recognized his reluctance to step up and take on new challenges. He saw moping and complaining and withholding and evading.

As the night wore on, Mark began to question the internal narrative about his boss that constantly ran in his mind. *If she's so obviously the villain I'm claiming her to be,* he wondered, *why do I have to spend so much internal energy trying to convince myself of it?* As he thought about this, it occurred to him that the narrative itself affected how he interacted with and treated his boss. *What if what I've been telling myself isn't true?* he wondered. The question was enough to get him out of bed.

He grabbed a yellow legal pad and drew a line down the center of the page. In the left-hand column, he began listing the ways that he really hadn't been helpful to his boss—the ways he had mistreated her and set her up for failure and disappointment. His list reached halfway down the page. Then on the right-hand side he began to write the ways that he could help. This list filled multiple pages. With each page turn, he felt a shackle coming off. As he stared at the ideas that had come flooding out of him, Mark realized that the person primarily responsible for holding him back had been himself. The realization freed him. A world of new possibility dawned in his mind.

When Mark returned to work, he began implementing some of the changes he had written. As he did so, he discovered that what his boss's boss had said to him was true: not only did the organization need more from Mark, he was capable of much more. He was not the victim he had been playing. Was his boss sometimes difficult? Yes. Did Mark still sometimes feel mistreated? Again, yes. Notwithstanding this, he realized that he had been using these issues as justifications for his own lack of effort. Some of the challenges he faced were real, but his constraints were mostly his own. He had always been free to do more and better.

Mark says that this experience was a career changer for him. He likely would not be where he is today had his mentor not cared about and believed enough in Mark *and* the company to tell him the truth about his performance and to invite him to do more.

With a renewed level of self-accountability, Mark began to flourish in his job. He began taking on more and more responsibilities, and his abilities grew with his performance. Within a year, this growth had prepared Mark for a great opportunity with one of the firm's healthcare clients. His experience at that healthcare company equipped him with the industry understanding that eventually enabled him to cofound his own company—an organization that has enriched the lives of millions.

Consider the central question that emerged from Mark's story: *What can I do to be more helpful?*

What can I do to be more helpful at work? What can I do to be more helpful at home? What can I do to be more helpful to those I know and to those I don't? What can I do? And will I see myself and others in ways that will enable me to do what I can do?

An indication of an outward mindset is the willingness of a person to honestly ask these questions in each area of his or her life, coupled with an excitement to begin acting on the answers despite challenges. If you consider the stories we have shared in this book, from Chip and his SWAT squad mixing baby bottles, to Alan Mulally saving Ford, to the woman who felt the desire to keep reaching out to her brother after his release from prison, you will see both this question and this energy at work.

So what will *you* do as you consider the people you work with and the people at home?

Consider what we have discussed. Whatever you do, you can do it with either an inward mindset or an outward mindset. Which way you do it will determine to a large degree your results.

- Start with mindset. Apply the outward-mindset pattern, SAM: see others, adjust efforts, and measure impact (chapters 9, 10, and 12).

- Don't wait for others to change. The most important move is to turn your mindset regardless of whether others change theirs (chapter 11).

- Mobilize yourself and your team or organization to achieve a collective goal (chapter 13).

- Allow people (beginning with yourself) to be fully responsible. Own your work—your plans, your actions, and your impact—and position others to own theirs (chapter 14).

- Eliminate the unnecessary distinctions that create distance between yourself and others (chapter 15).

- To the extent you have authority to do so, rethink systems and processes to turn them outward; create an organizational ecosystem that energizes people rather than manages objects (chapter 16).

- Implement an outward-mindset game plan. Commit to a regular cadence of outward-mindset activities, even if it's only a few minutes at a time (chapter 17).

We hope that for you this book has provided a service like the service provided to Mark Ballif by his mentor. If you have thought, *I can do better than I have been doing*, then the book will have been worth the read.

So what have you been seeing and thinking? And more importantly, what are you going to do about it?

We hope you have enjoyed reading *The Outward Mindset*. We have provided additional resources online, including a mindset audit tool that enables you to discover the degree to which you and your organization may be operating from an outward mindset. Additionally, many of the people we have written about in this book have graciously allowed us to film them and their organizations. If you would like to learn more from them, you can watch them share the details of their experiences at www.outwardmindset.com.

NOTES

Preface

1. Nate Boaz and Erica Ariel Fox, "Change Leader, Change Thyself," McKinley *Quarterly*, March 2014.

Chapter 2

1. Nate Boaz and Erica Ariel Fox, "Change Leader, Change Thyself," *McKinsey Quarterly*, March 2014.
2. Joanna Barsh and Johanne Lavoie, "Lead at Your Best," *McKinsey Quarterly*, April 2014.

Chapter 3

1. To explore Martin Buber's work for yourself, see Martin Buber, *I and Thou*, trans. Walter Kaufmann (New York: Charles Scribner's Sons, 1970).

Chapter 6

1. For a detailed exploration of the subject of justification and how the need for it arises, see one or both of our earlier books, *Leadership and Self-Deception* and *The Anatomy of Peace*.

Chapter 8

1. Sarah Green Carmichael, "The Debt Collection Company That Helps You Get a Job," *Harvard Business Review*, August 16, 2013.
2. Ibid.
3. Ibid.
4. Scott Davis, "Gregg Popovich Broke Down What He Looks for in Players, and It Was an Inspiring Life Lesson," *Business Insider*, February 22, 2016.

5. Michael Lee Stallard, "NBA's Spurs Culture Creates Competitive Advantage," FOXBusiness, February 25, 2015.
6. Ibid.
7. Ibid.

Chapter 9
1. If you want to learn more about Alan Mulally and what he and his team did to save Ford, we highly recommend Bryce G. Hoffman's excellent book, *American Icon: Alan Mulally and the Fight to Save Ford Motor Company* (New York: Crown Business, 2012).
2. Hoffman, *American Icon*, 109.
3. Ibid., 106–107.
4. Ibid., 111.
5. Ibid., 122.
6. Ibid., 125.

Chapter 10
1. Brenda Ueland, *Strength to Your Sword Arm: Selected Writings* (Duluth, MN: Holy Cow! Press, 1996), 205.
2. Ibid., 206.

Chapter 13
1. Hoffman, *American Icon*, 71.

Chapter 14
1. Hannah Arendt, *The Human Condition*, 2nd ed. (Chicago: University of Chicago Press, 1998).

Chapter 15
1. Richard Sheridan, *Joy, Inc.* (New York: Portfolio/Penguin, 2013), 42.

LIST OF STORIES

- Joe Bartley tucking in his daughter Anna, 63–64

Chapter 8
- Navy SEALs and the importance of an outward mindset, 65
- Bill Bartmann and the debt-collection agency CFS2, 67–69
- The San Antonio Spurs and their outward-mindset culture, 69–71

Chapter 9
- Alan Mulally and the Ford turnaround, 74–81

Chapter 10
- Shortening a power company's capital budgeting process, 83–85
- Brenda Ueland at parties, 86–87
- Rob Dillon of Dillon Floral learning to love customer visits, 87–89
- Playing hide-and-seek with the misbehaving boy, 89–92
- Attorney Charles Jackson returning money to his clients, 92–94
- Hope Arising determining an outward-mindset metric for clean water delivery in Ethiopia, 94–96

Chapter 11
- Jack Hauck, Larry Heitz, Al Klien, and Tubular Steel, 97–98, 100–104

Chapter 12
- KCPD officer Matt Tomasic being protected from a dangerous suspect by community members, 111
- Matt Tomasic leading change on the West Side of Kansas City, Missouri, 111–115
- A company resolving a labor-management dispute to avoid arbitration, 115–116

INDEX

ABOUT THE ARBINGER INSTITUTE

The Arbinger Institute delivers training, consulting, coaching, and digital tools to help individuals and organizations change mindset, transform culture, accelerate collaboration and innovation, resolve conflict, and sustainably improve results.

Arbinger's first book, *Leadership and Self-Deception*, originally published in 2000, is one of the top fifty bestselling leadership books of all time. Its sequel, *The Anatomy of Peace*, first published in 2006, has been number one or two on the Amazon bestseller list in the War and Peace and Conflict Resolution categories for more than a decade. This means that every hour of every day for over ten years, *The Anatomy of Peace* has been the bestselling book in its category. Few books in history can make that claim. *The Outward Mindset*, first published in 2016, shows how to successfully implement the ideas from *Leadership and Self-Deception* and *The Anatomy of Peace* in organizations and how to move individuals, teams, and organizations from in-the-box inward-mindset orientations to out-of-the-box outward-mindset orientations. Individually and together, these books help readers see their lives and work situations in entirely new ways and discover practical and powerful solutions to problems they were sure were someone else's.

As a result of its thirty-five-year track record with clients, Arbinger is now recognized as a world leader in the areas of mindset change, leadership, team building, conflict resolution, strategy, and culture change. Arbinger's clients range from individuals who are seeking help in their lives to many of the largest companies and governmental institutions in the world.

Worldwide interest in Arbinger's work has propelled the growth of Arbinger across the globe. Headquartered in the United States, Arbinger now has offices in nearly thirty countries, including throughout the Americas, Europe, Africa, the Middle East, India, Oceania, and Asia.

Arbinger's Mission and Process

The Arbinger Institute's mission is to turn the world outward—to help individuals, teams, and organizations get out of the inward-mindset box and become more connected, aware, and attentive to the needs, objectives, and challenges of colleagues, neighbors, family members, and even rivals. We work with organizations both large and small, well known and out of the spotlight. Our clients include many of the largest and most successful public, private, and governmental organizations in the world.

In our work with clients, we follow a three-step process: (1) mindset change, (2) leader development, and (3) systems improvement. Before engaging, we assess organizational performance to get a baseline from which to determine best courses of action and against which to measure client progress. To get this baseline, we utilize key organizational metrics and administer Arbinger's Mindset Assessment instrument. We then educate employees by equipping them through training with the following sets of outward-mindset implementation tools: self-awareness tools, mindset-change tools, accountability tools, collaboration tools, and (for managers) leadership tools. These tools set up an implementation game plan that we then help leaders and team members enact. We track progress and adjust the implementation game plan by conducting reassessments at regular intervals. We sustain progress by building up internal expertise and helping organizational leaders turn systems and processes outward so that they incentivize and reward working with an outward mindset rather than working with an inward mindset. This work ranges from strategic planning to systems reengineering to mentoring and executive coaching.

Sustained growth cannot come from expertise that resides outside an organization. While short-term growth sometimes can be purchased that way, ongoing sustained growth cannot be outsourced. An organization will rise only as far as its own people are equipped to take it. For these reasons, Arbinger's aim is to position and equip our clients with enough understanding and expertise in Arbinger's outward-mindset tools and processes to be able to "consult themselves" over time.

Arbinger embeds its expertise within client organizations in part by preparing and certifying internal experts to deliver Arbinger programs within their organizations. To learn more about Arbinger's training and consulting services, find out how to become an Arbinger facilitator within your organization, or explore other Arbinger publications and access client case studies, please visit www.arbinger.com or contact us by phone at our US headquarters at 801-447-9244.

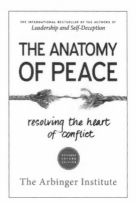

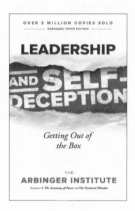

Berrett–Koehler
Publishers

Berrett-Koehler is an independent publisher dedicated to an ambitious mission: *Connecting people and ideas to create a world that works for all.*

Our publications span many formats, including print, digital, audio, and video. We also offer online resources, training, and gatherings. And we will continue expanding our products and services to advance our mission.

We believe that the solutions to the world's problems will come from all of us, working at all levels: in our society, in our organizations, and in our own lives. Our publications and resources offer pathways to creating a more just, equitable, and sustainable society. They help people make their organizations more humane, democratic, diverse, and effective (and we don't think there's any contradiction there). And they guide people in creating positive change in their own lives and aligning their personal practices with their aspirations for a better world.

And we strive to practice what we preach through what we call "The BK Way." At the core of this approach is *stewardship,* a deep sense of responsibility to administer the company for the benefit of all of our stakeholder groups, including authors, customers, employees, investors, service providers, sales partners, and the communities and environment around us. Everything we do is built around stewardship and our other core values of *quality, partnership, inclusion,* and *sustainability.*

This is why Berrett-Koehler is the first book publishing company to be both a B Corporation (a rigorous certification) and a benefit corporation (a for-profit legal status), which together require us to adhere to the highest standards for corporate, social, and environmental performance. And it is why we have instituted many pioneering practices (which you can learn about at www.bkconnection.com), including the Berrett-Koehler Constitution, the Bill of Rights and Responsibilities for BK Authors, and our unique Author Days.

We are grateful to our readers, authors, and other friends who are supporting our mission. We ask you to share with us examples of how BK publications and resources are making a difference in your lives, organizations, and communities at www.bkconnection.com/impact.

Dear reader,

Thank you for picking up this book and welcome to the worldwide BK community! You're joining a special group of people who have come together to create positive change in their lives, organizations, and communities.

What's BK all about?

Our mission is to connect people and ideas to create a world that works for all.

Why? Our communities, organizations, and lives get bogged down by old paradigms of self-interest, exclusion, hierarchy, and privilege. But we believe that can change. That's why we seek the leading experts on these challenges—and share their actionable ideas with you.

A welcome gift

To help you get started, we'd like to offer you a **free copy** of one of our bestselling ebooks:

www.bkconnection.com/welcome

When you claim your **free ebook**, you'll also be subscribed to our blog.

Our freshest insights

Access the best new tools and ideas for leaders at all levels on our blog at ideas.bkconnection.com.

Sincerely,

Your friends at Berrett-Koehler

Certified

Corporation